# MINDFUL AI

*REFLECTIONS ON*

*ARTIFICIAL INTELLIGENCE*

*(THE AI THOUGHT BOOK Reloaded)*

Murat Durmus

**ISBN**: 9798360396796 - **Imprint**: Independently published

**About the Author**

Murat Durmus is CEO and founder of AISOMA. A Frankfurt am Main (Germany) based company specializing in AI-based technology development and consulting. Besides being an entrepreneur, he devotes most of his time to philosophy and AI's impacts on society.

Contact: murat.durmus@aisoma.de

Cover Photo (Meditating Robot): © Can Stock Photo / sarah5

More Books by the Author on Amazon:

- **"INSIDE ALAN TURING: QUOTES & CONTEMPLATIONS"** (ISBN-13: 979-8751495848)
- **"Quantum Computing & Artificial Intelligence - The Perfect Match?"** (ISBN-13: 979-8464587502)

For

**Aynur,**

**Emre & Esra**

*(Thanks for your patience)*

# TABLE OF CONTENTS

# PREFACE

I sit in front of my notebook and try to write a preface. After all the thoughts and quotes I've written over the past few years, I'm struggling for words. Honestly, I have yet to think of writing a book about the outpourings of my neurons on the topic of AI. However, the reactions and feedback on social media and the requests of some of my friends were so positive that they finally convinced me to publish it.

Even as a young boy, I had a penchant for snippets of thoughts and quotes. I remember devouring Marcus Aurelius' "Meditations," and they still inspire me more than 20 years later. They make me think and feel like I can penetrate related topics more deeply. To me, quotes are like thought drops that sometimes penetrate deep into our souls and give us insights that a hundred books can't.

If this book inspires you or makes you look at the subject of artificial intelligence from different angles, then it has fully served its purpose and, at the same time, made me one of the happiest people in this world.

I hope you enjoy reading it and that it gives you a lot of inspiration and insights.

✾✾✾

Be *Mindful* with Artificial Intelligence,

otherwise, it will overtake you one day.

Murat Durmus –

Frankfurt am Main, October 2022

## THOUGHT & QUOTES

---

# ARTIFICIAL INTELLIGENCE

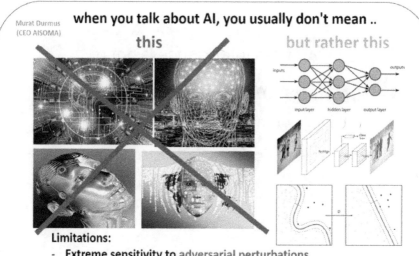

Murat Durmus
(CEO AISOMA)

when you talk about AI, you usually don't mean ..

this

but rather this

**Limitations:**
- **Extreme sensitivity to** adversarial perturbations
- **Extreme sensitivity to** any input change **not seen in the training data**
- **It can only make sense of** what it has seen before

I have done a terrible thing.

I have demystified Artificial Intelligence.

Recognizing that two points of data are

connected is not enough.

The System must ask

**why** one point affects another.

Artificial Intelligence is not a

new wave of technology.

It is much more like a **Tsunami** that

threatens to flood us if we are not mindful.

➢ AI is a branch of philosophy and not of computer science.
➢ AI is not a revolutionary but a transforming technology.
➢ We have only seen & experienced the tip of the iceberg in AI.
➢ AI is an accelerator of evolution.

➤ AI makes us seriously question what it means to be a human.

❀❀❀

## Progress

What worries me a bit is that we don't know the current state of AI progress. New heights and approaches are reported and published almost daily from all parts of the world. Hardly any area seems to be untouched. Sure, we all want progress, but really at any cost? I think a little more humility in the development of AI would do the whole thing well; otherwise, the whole thing threatens to overwhelm us one day, and we will no longer be able to correct it, let alone control it.

❀❀❀

## Robustness

The foremost question we should always ask ourselves when we get serious about AI:

*"How can we make robust artificial intelligence systems in the face of lack of knowledge about the world?"*

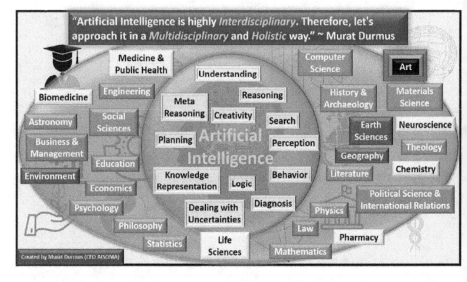

Artificial Intelligence is highly Interdisciplinary. Therefore, let's approach it in a **Multidisciplinary** & **Holistic** way

## Multidisciplinary

The lack of domain-specific knowledge when designing AI Models:

One of the main reasons many rely on black-box models is not the model's accuracy and performance but merely the lack of domain-specific knowledge. The problem could be solved by training more experts in a specific domain, such as medicine, biology, psychology, pharmacy, marketing, etc., to Data-Scientists or ML-Engineers. At least to the extent that they can evaluate the whole and adapt it if necessary. There are already some, but it needs to be challenged and promoted much more. We can only benefit most from AI if we approach it in a multidisciplinary way.

## Robustness of Artificial Intelligence Systems:

Steadily increasing technological advances in artificial intelligence encourage more and more businesses and governments to deploy AI in high-stakes environments, including autonomous driving, diagnostics in medicine, managing the power grid, and controlling autonomous weapons systems. However, for such applications, AI methods must be robust to the known unknowns (the uncertain aspects of the world that the computer can reason about explicitly) and the unknown unknowns (the elements of the world that system models do not capture). Thus, we need to pay more attention to the challenges of dealing with both known and, above all, the unknown unknowns. These issues are essential because they address the fundamental question of how finite systems can survive in a complex and dangerous world and thrive for humankind and nature's benefit.

From pre-existing bias to biased datasets to the emergence of unpredictable correlations; The reasons are manifold. It will still take a while for AI to reach a certain level of maturity.

**Brute-Force-AI**

Did you know that GPT-3[1] has trained on 8 million text documents (data that reflect biases that occur in the real world) scraped from the web, costing $12 million in electricity to train it?

I call such an approach: "Irresponsible Brute-Force-AI."

***AI, for AI's sake, is a nearly-guaranteed path to disaster***

!❀❀❀

Uninterpretable (Black-Box) algorithms should only be used for knowledge discovery processes and not for decision-making.

---

[1] Generative Pre-trained Transformer 3 (GPT-3) is an autoregressive language model that uses deep learning to produce human-like text. It is the third-generation language prediction model in the GPT-n series created by OpenAI, [GPT-3 (n.d.). In Wikipedia. Retrieved June 11, 2020, from https://en.wikipedia.org/wiki/GPT-3]

## Race of AI

The question of who will win the race and dominate AI in the future is primarily not about who has the leading companies or produces the cutting-edge innovative technology in this sector. It is rather about who has companies that can quickly take over the breakthrough algorithms/technologies and adapt them to processes that create economic (and hopefully sustainable) value.

The adoption of Artificial Intelligence must be done holistically and not in fragmented components that are not fully integrated into the Organizations.

One should focus on Data, not on Algorithms

**AI Depression**

I am suffering a bit from AI depression.

Let me give you some reasons:

▶ The AI-Control-Problem (still not sufficiently solved)

▶ Still significant concerns about privacy, ethical issues, and security

▶ No uniform/sluggish regulations and laws.

▶ The reality and expectations of AI diverge significantly; AI is overhyped.

▶ Ethical/psychological implications are not yet clear; much is still a theory and not proven in practice.

▶ Philosophical, sociological, and psychological human-science studies/approaches are still not appreciated enough.

▶ The hype is followed by sobriety (AI is still an expert system)

▶ Many AI systems are still inefficient, need a lot of energy, or must be implemented complicatedly. We need different, more efficient approaches.

▶ Data awareness has not yet developed sufficiently across the world.

▶ Still too little usable (real-time) data is generated. The significant expansion of Edge/IoT/5G devices and infrastructures will continue.

▶ AI is dominated by a few Big-Techs (AI is becoming a power instrument increasingly); This could have adverse effects on AI.

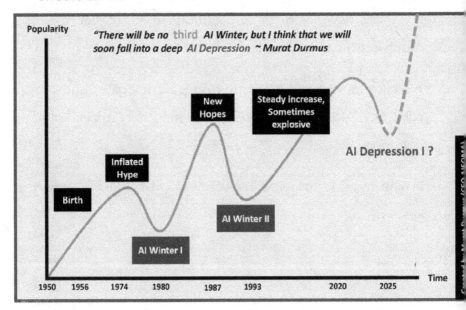

The field of AI is highly

***interdisciplinary*** & ***evolutionary***.

The more AI penetrates our life and

environment, the more comprehensive

the points we have to consider and

adapt. Technological developments are

far ahead ethical & philosophical

interpretations.

This fact is disturbing,

## The AI-Control-Problem

In my opinion, the AI Control Problem is still underestimated and receives too little attention. Only when we have found a satisfactory solution for the control problem should we allow AI to interfere fully in our lives and not before.

There is still a long way to go.

Major approaches to the control problem include alignment, which aims to align AI goal systems with human values, and capability control, which seeks to reduce an AI system's capacity to harm humans or gain power. However, capability control proposals are generally not considered reliable or sufficient to solve the control problem but rather as potentially valuable supplements to alignment efforts.

Some researchers try to imitate the human brain with digital machines. In my opinion, the wrong approach. It would be more promising with a mixture of digital and analog machines.

Artificial Intelligence is still a big grab bag. Nobody knows precisely in which direction the journey will go. But one thing is sure: We have seen only the tip of the iceberg so far.

Artificial intelligence fires the imagination of many people. But, unfortunately, also that of the foolish.

※※※

## Deep Learning

With all the great successes we have already achieved with Deep Learning, we must not forget one thing:

Deep learning is still inefficient compared to some "classical" methods (developed over centuries by brilliant people). Deep Learning is more of a "sledgehammer to crack a nut" method. **We need more efficient approaches**.

※※※

**Many People ask me why I'm so addicted to AI:**

It is the interdisciplinary component that attracts me to Artificial Intelligence.

## 8 Definitions of Artificial Intelligence

The following are eight well-known definitions of artificial intelligence:

"**[The automation of] activities that we associate with human thinking, activities such as decision-making, problem-solving, learning ...**"

(Bellman, 1978)

"**The exciting new effort to make computers think ... machines with minds, in the full and literal sense**"

(Haugeland 1985)

"**The study of mental faculties through the use of computational models.**"

(Chamiak and McDermott, 1985)

"**The art of creating machines that perform functions that require intelligence when performed by people.**"

(Kurzweil, 1990)

"**The study of how to make computers do things at which, at the moment, people are better.**"

(Ritch and Knight, 1991)

**"The study of the computations that make it possible to perceive, reason, and act."**

(Winston 1992)

**"Computational Intelligence is the study of the design of intelligent agents."**

(Poole at al. 1998)

**"AI ... is concerned with intelligent behavior in artefacts."**

(Nilsson, 1998)

*Source: (Russell and Norvig 2016)*

**I have an AI joke, but it is biased.**

I'm sitting here thinking about AI. So many new papers, progress, and achievements every week. Simply impossible to keep track of; There seem to be no boundaries when it comes to AI. Technologically, AI is being pushed from all sides and integrated into almost every aspect of our lives. But as far as the ethical, sociological, philosophical, and psychological aspects are concerned, we are more or less treading water. Don't get me wrong, there is much excellent work in these areas, but I get the feeling that it is not taken seriously enough (especially by the big techs). Everything they do in this area seems like tokenism. Developing a new and better algorithm appears easier than creating an ethical concept and integrating it. Unfortunately, the latter affects many areas, such as corporate culture, philosophy, organization, etc. Here, in contrast to technological and mathematical challenges, one must fight against human barriers and dogmas; One feels like Sisyphus.

It's a feeling, and I can be wrong in this respect.

# AI ETHICS

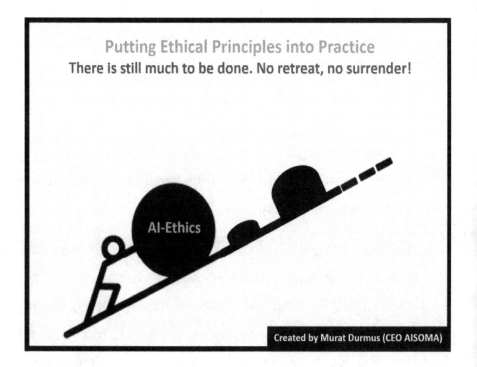

Putting Ethical Principles into Practice
There is still much to be done. No retreat, no surrender!

AI-Ethics

Created by Murat Durmus (CEO AISOMA)

Discussions about AI Ethics are still primarily conducted in academic circles. But one can already see that many companies are earnestly dealing with it. One thing that seems clear to me:

Graduates of Philosophy and Ethics will be in high demand in the future to investigate AI-related processes through a human lens

❀❀❀

From a technological point of view, my wish for the year 2023 is that AI ethics is taken more seriously and its use in practice is pushed more.

AI is changing our lives in challenging ways to predict and, for many, to understand. If technology is to be more socially responsible in the future, we need to invest much more in AI ethics education; This would inevitably lead to many more AI ethics jobs. Furthermore, every company that uses artificial intelligence should employ an AI ethics officer. AI ethics must take a central place in AI education efforts. The more AI penetrates our life and environment, the more comprehensive the points we have to consider and adapt. Unfortunately, technological developments are far ahead of ethical and philosophical interpretations. The whole thing seems like a handful of philosophers versus an armada of technologists. We have to balance this imbalance if we do not want to be crushed and controlled by this technology in the future.

The more Artificial Intelligence

enters our lives,

the more essential

**Ethics** & **Philosophy**

become.

**The least we should do:**

Policymakers should not accept black-box models without examining alternative possibilities with models that can be interpreted and explained.

The Battle for the Supremacy of Artificial Intelligence has the potential to lead Humanity into the abyss.

❀❀❀

**Ethical guidelines, frameworks, and toolkits are not enough.**

Ethical guidelines, frameworks, and toolkits are insufficient; they can only address AI ethical problems selectively but not holistically. As AI becomes more advanced and widely used, we must create more social and institutional structures and spaces that encourage, guide, support, and sufficiently reward ethical behavior. These structures would greatly facilitate and motivate people to live and work more ethically.

**No Women, no Trustworthy AI!**

#diversitymatters

There are biased people (politicians, managers, etc.), companies, and institutions. For some time now, more and more biased algorithms have been designed.

Both are already wreaking havoc.

We can try to convince prejudiced people to eliminate their prejudices through education and persuasion.

The algorithms can be tried with different techniques to get rid of bias.

In this sense, we have not yet achieved anything. We replace one evil with another. We urgently need clear and uniform ethical guidelines that must be put into practice. Algorithms have one advantage over people: they do not take the whole thing personally or feel offended by their egos.

**Team Diversity**

In a world that is becoming more data-driven and algorithms are used more and more for decision-making, we need more **DIVERSITY**!

To avoid data bias, it is not only the variety of data sets that is sufficient but the diversity of the team should be expanded. More group diversity means that people with different perspectives, experiences, and cultures can supply the data points.

One thing is sure: Diversity in teams will positively affect the machine learning models created, as the teams will be able to understand and interpret the requirements and outcomes much better.

## Uniform Regulation

We need a uniform regulation for AI that is valid worldwide. In the long run, it makes no sense for each country, company, and organization to do its own thing. Most AI applications are and will be used globally.

Don't be scared of racist people. Be frightened of **'racist'** algorithms because they have no conscience and are much more effective.

It is a bit absurd and incomprehensible that some people and companies still need to be convinced of the importance of ethical principles and guidelines for the coming age of automation and algorithmic decision-making.

Team Diversity is the easiest and, at the same time, one of the most effective means of reducing bias.

**Operationalization of AI-Ethics**

The operationalization of AI-Ethics should have the highest priority and needs to be promoted more strongly. If we do not manage to implement ethical principles in real-world applications shortly, this area is in danger of disappearing or losing its seriousness. Therefore, technological and ethical developments must go hand in hand.

Meanwhile, many possibilities exist to design an algorithm that is fairer, more explainable, and bias-free. But ethical AI starts with the human being himself, and he bears the primary responsibility. We should not concentrate exclusively on tooling but rather train those who develop these models better. AI-Experts and Philosophers must come closer.

###

## Ethical AI in practice: Five points to consider

1.   Update governance processes to minimize risk and address uncertainty

2.   Take action so all employees can participate in an AI-powered workplace

3.   Improve data and diversity to eliminate unfair bias

4.    Increase data security and privacy to boost consumer trust

5.      Put trust in the hands of customers by explaining AI

## Ethical design and use of AI-Systems

The ethical design and use of AI-Systems require a multidisciplinary team effort. It demands the active collaboration of the entire team in maintaining a deeply rooted culture of responsibility and establishing a governance architecture that applies ethical practices at every stage of the implementation life-cycle.

## AI Regulation

Too strict regulation slows down the use and innovative power of Artificial Intelligence. Whereas without sufficient supervision, AI threatens to overwhelm us. We should do everything we can to ensure that both go hand in hand—a big challenge and dilemma.

## Why AI Ethics is so challenging

As an AI ethicist, one must have profound knowledge in many areas. You have to be familiar with the technology, the underlying philosophy, the ethical and moral aspects, and its psychological and sociological implications for humans, the environment, and society. Not to forget the legal and privacy challenges; last but not least, you should have methodological knowledge and conceptual skills to translate the requirements into a framework to implement them in practice.

Most people who advocate for transparent, fair, and 'ethical' AI are aware that we have neglected or ignored these issues in many areas of technology, business, and research. Hence, many AI Ethicists are motivated to get it right from the start, at least when it comes to AI, knowing that AI will touch and transform all areas of our lives in the future.

AI ethics is highly interdisciplinary and dynamic. For me, it is one of the most essential, exciting, and promising fields of activity for the future.

**AI Ethics Definitions**

The following are four definitions of AI ethics.

Which one do you think is the most accurate?

Are definitions helpful, or should they be dispensed with?

1. "*AI ethics is a set of values, principles, and techniques that employ widely accepted standards of right and wrong to guide moral conduct in the development and use of AI technologies.*"

- (The Alan Turing Institute)

2. "*AI ethics is a system of moral principles and techniques intended to inform the development and responsible use of artificial intelligence technology.*"

 - (whatis.techtarget.com)

3. "*AI ethics is the multi-disciplinary and multistakeholder field of study that aims to define and implement technical and non-technical solutions to address these concerns and mitigate the risks.*"

- (World Economic Forum)

4. "*A systematic normative reflection, based on a holistic, comprehensive, multicultural and evolving framework of interdependent values, principles and actions that can guide societies in dealing responsibly with the known and unknown impacts of AI technologies on human beings, societies and the environment and ecosystems, and offers them a basis to accept or reject AI technologies*."

- (UNESCO)

Note:

I know that one cannot adequately define terms like AI, ethics, and consciousness so that everyone agrees with them. But we need descriptions with definitional characters to create a basis for discussion.

## Ethics Guidelines

Most National AI-Ethics Guidelines are not practical. They are focusing too much on high-level principles. We need use-case-specific ethics by design approaches. From the Idea, design, implementation, and roll-out, ethics and its implications to society must be considered at all stages of the implementation. Furthermore, ethics must be proactive and prepare for what could go wrong and not what has already gone wrong and caused harm.

֍֍֍

Why the most AI-Ethicists are so motivated

Most of those who advocate for transparent, fair, and 'ethical' AI are aware that we have neglected or ignored these issues in many areas of technology, business, and research. Hence, many AI Ethicists are motivated to get it right from the beginning, at least when it comes to AI. Knowing that AI will touch and transform all areas of our lives in the future.

*"We need more people with vital computational statistics and machine learning skills who do not come from computer science, math, or physics backgrounds but human-, social-, life- or environmental sciences; This would immensely enrich and benefit the developments of AI."*

**Ethical impacts of Artificial Intelligence**

**Social impacts:** the potential impact of AI on the labor market and economy and how different demographic groups might be affected. It addresses questions of inequality and the risk that AI will further concentrate power and wealth in a few hands. Issues related to privacy, human rights, and dignity are addressed, as are risks that AI will perpetuate the biases, intended or otherwise, of existing social systems or their creators. This section also raises questions about the impact of AI technologies on democracy, suggesting that these technologies may operate for the benefit of state-controlled economies

**Psychological impacts:** what impacts might arise from human-robot relationships? How might we address dependency and deception? Should we consider whether robots deserve to be given the status of 'personhood' and the legal and moral implications of doing so?

**Financial system impacts:** The potential impacts of AI on financial systems are considered, including risks of manipulation and collusion and the need to build accountability.

**Legal system impacts:** There are several ways AI could affect the legal system, including questions relating to crime, such as liability if an AI is used for criminal activities and the extent to which AI might support criminal activities such as drug trafficking. In situations where an AI is involved in personal injuries, such as in a collision involving an autonomous vehicle, questions arise around the legal approach to claims (whether it is a case of negligence), which is usually the basis for vehicular claims accidents or product liability).

**Environmental impacts**: increasing use of AIs come with the increased use of natural resources, increased energy demands, and waste disposal issues. However, AIs could improve the way we manage waste and resources, leading to environmental benefits.

**Impacts on trust: society** relies on trust. For AI to take on tasks, such as surgery, the public will need to trust the technology. Trust includes aspects such as fairness (that AI will be impartial), transparency (that we will be able to understand how an AI arrived at a particular decision), accountability (someone can be held accountable for mistakes made by AI) and control (how we might 'shut down' an AI that becomes too powerful).

## Building blocks of a course for aspiring AI-Ethicists

I've been thinking about what the building blocks of a course for aspiring AI-Ethicists might look like; It becomes apparent that AI ethicists' activities are highly interdisciplinary and challenging.

The points serve as a suggestion and you are welcome to suggest further points in the comments.

◆ History and Philosophy of AI

◆ Key concepts and types of AI (Machine Learning)

- Supervised Learning
- Unsupervised Learning
- Semi-Supervised Learning
- Self-Supervised Learning
- Reinforcement Learning
- Strong & Weak AI
- Difference between classical programming, statistics, and machine learning

◆ Data Awareness & Literacy

◆ Data Ethics Concepts

◆ The future of AI (what can we expect)

◆ Ethical Theories

- Utilitarian
- Rights-based ethics

◆ Ethical implications of AI

◆ Technology and the Greater Human Good

◆ Core ethical principles

- Diversity, non-discrimination, and fairness
- Transparency
- Accountability
- Explainability
- Human agency and oversight
- Technical robustness and safety
- Privacy and data governance
- Societal and environmental wellbeing

◆ Gender transformative operationalization of ai principles

◆ Human Rights & AI

◆ Cognitive Biases

◆ Types of Algorithmic Bias

◆ How to investigate and identify bias in algorithmic decisions

◆ Challenges of explainability & interpretability

◆ Privacy (Privacy-Preserving Machine Learning/Federated Learning)

◆ Ethical and moral issues associated with the development and implementation of AI

◆ How to design AI GDPR Compliant

◆ AI Regulation

◆ The criminal potential of AI

◆ The psychological and sociological aspects of AI

◆ Investigating Human-Machine interaction

◆ Concepts for ethical AI in education

◆ Human & Nature Centric AI

◆ Economics of Intelligent Automation

◆ How to put AI Ethics into practice

◆ Artificial Intelligence & Law

◆ Measuring & auditing AI applications

# EXPLAINABLE AI (XAI)

Demonstrating explanations only for the correct method or class is misleading and insufficient. Furthermore, this approach can create false confidence in the explanation method and the black box. This situation can occur when saliency maps (In computer vision, a saliency map is an image that shows each pixel's unique quality) are the explanations because they tend to highlight edges, thus providing similar answers for each class. These explanations could be identical even if the model is always wrong.

## Algorithmic Transparency

Algorithmic transparency may help mitigate ethical issues such as fairness or accountability, but it also creates ethically essential risks. Too much openness in the wrong context can destroy the positive development of AI-enabled processes. Everyone should know that the idea of fully transparent algorithms should be weighed carefully. We still have significant challenges ahead, as we have to find a balance between security and transparency considerations for each specific developed AI-based System.

❀❀❀

If a black-box solution has solved a problem, the whole thing always has a particular disadvantage because we don't know precisely how it solved the problem. Therefore, we need explainable and transparent AI.

❀❀❀

Explainability is one thing; interpreting it rightly (for the good of society), is another.

Explainable AI is only an intermediate goal and should not be proclaimed as the ultimate goal. The real challenge is to interpret it rightly for society's good; precisely for this, we need more philosophers, psychologists, sociologists, and comparable human scientists. transparent AI.

### Diversity and Bias

To avoid data bias, it is not only the variety of data sets that is sufficient but the diversity of the team should be expanded. More team diversity means that people with many perspectives and different experiences/cultures can supply the data points.

One thing is sure: diversity in teams will have a very positive effect on the ML Models created, as the teams will be able to understand and interpret the requirements/outcomes better

## Dealing with AI Bias

If you are dealing with AI-Bias, you usually face these four challenges:

**1. Unknown unknowns**

**2. Incomplete processes**

**3. Lack of relevant context**

and last but not least

**4. The definition of fairness**

Unfortunately, all the points pose a big challenge. Especially the latter.

# PHILOSOPHY

## Why the field of AI needs more Philosophers

We are all confronted with ethical questions every day and are often overwhelmed by them. The Philosophers are not much different. They are usually better at analyzing and occasionally solving them, but they cannot always provide fail-safe techniques. However, what philosophy can do very well is offer a disciplined way to think about ethical issues and identify hidden moral assumptions to establish principles by which our actions can be guided and ultimately judged for society's good.

❀❀❀

## Philosophers

I thought about what philosophers would say about the current AI. Below are four philosophers as examples. Feel free to add more.

**Leibniz**: Always develop the best of all possible models.

**Nietzsche**: If you deal with AI for too long, eventually, the AI will look inside you one day.

**Popper**: AI must be falsifiable.

**Kant**: Design only AI Systems to that maxim by which you can, at the same time, will that it should become a universal law.

❀❀❀

The AI Community needs more Dialectic than ever. Otherwise, this technology will surely overtake us one day.

❀❀❀

**Behaviorism**

The current AI approach of many Researchers and Engineers reminds me of Behaviorism, except in a more modern, computationally sophisticated form. It is highly doubtful that using statistical techniques (what ML is) to determine regularities in masses of data provides us with decisive insights into the question: What is intelligence? We are still groping in the dark.

❀❀❀

Philosophy is such a powerful Tool. One can get to the bottom of things by thinking alone and often dissolving them.

❀❀❀

**Data Science from the philosophical perspective**

Professor John McCarthy already recognized the great importance of philosophy (The Philosophy of AI and the AI of Philosophy[2]) for the field of AI. Unfortunately, we often get lost in technical details and neglect the holistic view of the field. The sum is much more different than its parts.

------------------------------

[2] The Philosophy of AI and the AI of Philosophy by Professor John McCarthy
http://jmc.stanford.edu/articles/aiphil2.html

# DATA & BUSINESS

> Companies and authorities that continue to ignore Artificial Intelligence or neglect to integrate it into their organizations and processes will pay a high price for it. They will no longer be competitive. They will drown in Data and Complexity because the world is becoming *more and more Data-Driven*. ~ Murat Durmus

Data is not the new Oil nor the new Electricity. Data (Information) is everything because we are drowning in it and only using a fraction of it so far. Imagine that the entire available treasure of data is lifted and made accessible. The possible applications that are offered exceed my imagination.

A company nowadays without an AI-Strategy is like a sailboat without a sail. So as far as the future is concerned, I think Data Awareness will be a crucial criterion for success. It doesn't matter what kind of activity you are dealing with.

❀❀❀

The more Data is generated, the more difficult it will be to identify functional patterns. Despite the tools already available, we are in grave danger of drowning in useless Data.

❀❀❀

There is too much focus on Algorithms in the industry. But the key is the Data

**Monetizing AI**

Most enterprises are striving to monetize AI in a variety of applications. However, this quest for profitable use of machine learning systems is not primarily driven by value- or principle-based ethics but, unfortunately, by economic ambitions.

🌀🌀🌀

Before companies seriously consider digitization, they should first develop a comprehensive Data Awareness; This is the only way to ensure that digitization is successful and, above all, sustainable.

🌀🌀🌀

We need more Data Engineers than AI-Experts because AI comes into play when the data is made available in an appealing form.

The fear of job loss through AI is omnipresent and justified, but it also has a positive aspect. We are forced to think more seriously about redefining work. And That's a good thing

## Thinking Data

We need to rethink our way of thinking about Data and its use. AI can only achieve its full potential if it has enough data. Data Protection & Privacy are critical, but we should make an exception, especially in the health sector. Think of all those who suffer and will suffer. It would be irresponsible not to use the full potential of AI.

One of the most common reasons for the failure of AI-Projects is: To make the statement: Our Company or Product uses AI,- many companies plunge into the world of AI without really thinking about whether AI makes sense or not.

**AI for AI's sake is a nearly-guaranteed path to disaster.**

❄❄❄

Process-Oriented Thinking will no longer be sufficient in the future. Instead, we have to go down some steps and design much more from the perspective of (raw) data to aain new and more meaninaful Insiahts.

❄❄❄

Noisy Data is to Artificial Intelligence what Dark Matter is to Physics. Understanding and handling both will play a vital role in future development in the respective fields.

## AI-Projects

One of the main reasons so many companies still need help initiating AI Projects is that AI Projects usually have an undefined project outcome. The results can be overwhelming or very disappointing. Uncertainties and probabilities still belong to many in casinos, not business projects and strategies. That must change because dealing with uncertainties and probabilities will be in the future one of the crucial factors of success.

The amount of data increases rapidly. As a result, the way we approach problem-solving is changing. We are in the midst of a transition phase; The responsibility and influence of Data Scientists and AI Experts are steadily increasing. That much is

# EDUCATION & FUTURE OF WORK

*Many are concerned about the lack of AI-Experts. The lack of 'real' Thinkers & Philosophers is even more alarming.*

In the future, learning at the moment will become a Modus Operandi, and the ability to acquire new knowledge will be valued much higher than the knowledge one already has. That much is certain.

❀❀❀

Storytelling with Data should become a compulsory subject at every level of education because Data Awareness will be a crucial factor for success in the future.

❀❀❀

**Academic Inflation**

We live in times of academic inflation. Unfortunately, most people focus only on getting titles and degrees. As a result, they usually develop tunnel vision and tunnel thinking and are no longer aware of how diverse life and knowledge are.

If things continue like this, you will soon need a Ph.D. to be a cashier at McDonald's.

*Don't grasp titles and degrees;*

*strive for multidisciplinary,*

*holistic knowledge and insights.*

The day will come when a degree in philosophy and ethics will be more in demand than a computer scientist or economist.

❀❀❀

**Experts**

Beware of the Wave of so Called "Experts "

I know that I know nothing.

We should all have the same attitude as Newton:

*"To myself, I am only a child playing on the beach, while vast oceans of truth lie undiscovered before me."*

- Sir Isaac Newton

❀❀❀

Before you study a specific subject, consider its historical background in detail; only then can you successfully penetrate it.

❀❀❀

**Interdisciplinary Thinking**

The 'problem' with Interdisciplinary Thinking is that almost everyone finds it relevant and significant when you ask people about it. But unfortunately, very few practice it or thoughtfully incorporate it into their work. Interdisciplinary thinking is not only meant for research but should be considered in all our activities.

Data Science contains the term Science. It seems to me that some practicing Data Scientists still haven't internalized this or are not aware of it. They should call themselves Data Wrangler, Data Munger, Algorithm Selector, or the like. The problem is, the titles don't sound that sexy.

The use of Artificial Intelligence is a superior form of delegating tasks;
without loss of control!

**A Leader without Vision is like a candle without a wick.**

## Probably the most valuable Tip for aspiring Data Scientists and ML-Engineers

You can take a Coursera or Udemy course, work through some practical tutorials with Jupyter Notebook, use fancy tools, have a collection of helpful Cheat Sheets and books, or have multiple certifications. All is well and good, but it doesn't mean you have a complete grasp of the subject.

Test your skills by implementing a use case from scratch. Without using any ready-made resources or instructions. From data collection, data preparation & understanding, modeling, training, and optimization to a robust pipeline. Be able to explain and interpret what you have realized. Try to visualize it and describe it to someone who is not n specialist in the field. Do this several times, and you will notice how what you have learned above will fuse into something unique and valuable.

Finally, I would like to elaborate on the following:

I have been asked the question below many times.

How do I become an AI-Expert?

**You can't.**

In my opinion, you can't be an expert in a rapidly developing field, and something new is presented almost daily. Furthermore, I think the term expert is highly questionable. I feel more like Newton when I deal with AI or other sciences:

*"To myself, I am only a child playing on the beach, while vast oceans of truth lie undiscovered before me."*

~ Isaac Newton

## A kind of Mantra

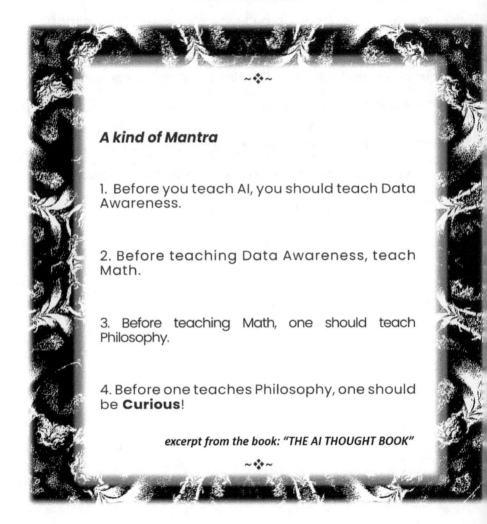

~❖~

*A kind of Mantra*

1. Before you teach AI, you should teach Data Awareness.

2. Before teaching Data Awareness, teach Math.

3. Before teaching Math, one should teach Philosophy.

4. Before one teaches Philosophy, one should be **Curious**!

*excerpt from the book: "THE AI THOUGHT BOOK"*

~❖~

# SOCIETY & HUMANITY

Recently, the term Human-Centric has appeared more often in connection with technological developments.

**What about Nature-Centric?**

I think some still underestimate the future impact of AI on society. AI is not a revolutionary technology but a transformative one. The implications will not be immediately apparent in the community and industry; they will be gradual and lasting. The engineers and the Big-Techs are pushing AI to higher and higher levels, while philosophers, sociologists, and psychologists are trying to keep up. There is some promising interdisciplinary cooperation, but on the whole, developments are running side by side rather than together. We must create more spaces and opportunities where both fields can work together more intensively and exchange ideas. Furthermore, we should be wary about "Ethics Washing," otherwise we will one day have unpleasant surprises.

**Building bridges**

In the long run, it makes no sense for philosophers to do their own thing and engineers their own. Too much is lost during the transfer. Therefore, building bridges is not enough. Both fields must merge.

It sounds unrealistic to most ... but this is precisely why we should accept the challenge and push it vigorously.

**More philosophy for Engineers!**

**More technology for Philosophers!**

This approach would increase our chances of successfully mastering the age of AI and automation immensely.

Artificial Intelligence is much more than just another promising technology. It makes us think more gravely about being human and ethical. And that's a good thing

The question will not be whether AI will one day be so advanced that it will be on the same level as human intelligence or far more advanced. The question will be whether or not we humans can evolve with AI. The AI is driven from all sides by brilliant people to higher and higher performances while humankind feels to be treading water. We have to develop significantly in philosophical, ethical, psychological, and sociological terms and fuse them into rapid technological developments if we do not want to experience any unpleasant surprises in the future.

I am concerned that humans will adapt more to artificial intelligence in the future than vice versa.

**AI Snowball**

Philosophers and "Experts" see AI as having many advantages for humanity, but at the same time, also dangers that are difficult to control and predict.

Nobody knows exactly where the journey will go and where it will end.

But one thing seems sure:

The snowball is getting bigger and bigger,

and the slope is getting steeper and steeper.

All AI is useless if it atrophies society.

That's why we need ethical principles. It's not just about AI but the people who 'must' interact with it.

We are in the midst of a transition period. The more advanced Artificial Intelligence becomes, the more uncertainty spreads. We must reposition ourselves and change our mindset if we don't want to perish.

# MIX

**ART**ificial **INTELLIGENCE** contains two notions that cannot be measured and not defined.

Autonomous Driving

To reach Level 5 in autonomous driving in the foreseeable future is a pure utopia, no matter what Tesla and Co. want to tell you. The expectations and reckless pursuits can take the AI into an abyss, if not into a frosty winter. Nevertheless, AI is still an expert system, and the open world is a No-go-Area, as long as we have not sufficiently solved the optimization- and the AI Control Problem.

Technology should never have the purpose of replacing or degrading us. Instead, its main goal should be to open new doors of insights to understand the Universe better and push the quality of life to a higher level. Everything else is just a means to an end.

Artificial Intelligence is sexy; The world is getting fitter and fitter. As a result, more trained models are finding their way into the most diverse areas of our lives.

Maybe we should treat confused groups, associations, and organizations on earth with the Gradient Boosting Algorithm because Gradient Boosting combines weak "learners" into a single strong learner in an iterative fashion.

Some worry that one day AI will dominate and enslave us. The debate seems hypocritical. Ruthless exploitation and pollution of our planet, wars, terrorism, oppression, child labor, poverty ... best of all possible worlds?

Ask G. W. Leibniz.

I fear the day that humans will be just another node beside all the other devices in a fully connected world: no own opinion, no critical questioning, and every thought and action calculated to the smallest detail.

The Turing Test is just a Simulation of Human Thinking with given limits. No more, no less. It says nothing about Intelligence.

❀❀❀

## Smart City

There are two ways to make the City Smarter.

1. Increasing the Common Sense of the urban population (more free books, education, cultural events, etc.)

2. Collecting Data with the Internet of Things (IoT) sensors to manage assets and resources efficiently;

Both should be vigorously pursued.

❀❀❀

**For a city to become a smart city,**

**it must first become a data city.**

❀❀❀

## Influencer

The main concern of an Influencer should firstly be to inspire the community and secondly to convey complex facts and technologies in a simple way to show their meaningful usage. The rest is negligible.

Probably the most promising AI Use-Case:

Fighting Natural Stupidity with Artificial Intelligence

❀❀❀

You can only make good coffee if you have suitable beans. The same applies to Machine Learning. Without enough or the correct data, your model will usually deliver disappointing results. The rest is more or less craftsmanship.

❀❀❀

**Q:** What is the main difference between a deep learning system and the human brain?

**A:** Most human brains have stopped learning.

❀❀❀

The signs are growing that we are living in a Simulation and that the Universe is a gigantic Holodeck.

If so, then the development of Superintelligence is only a matter of time.

I think the Nobel Prize Winners and Teams of the Future will have one thing in common. They will have an in-depth knowledge of Data Science.

We should free ourselves from the tight corset of causality and become more comfortable with probabilities and uncertainties because that will be the requirements of the future.

The Metaverse is the ideal playground
where the AI can let off steam.
The more humans lose themselves in it,
the more AI will take control.
That much is certain.

# A BRIEF HISTORY OF ARTIFICIAL INTELLIGENCE

Artificial intelligence (AI) is a growing discipline of sixty years that encompasses a range of sciences, theories, and techniques (including mathematical logic, statistics, probabilities, computational neurobiology, computer science, and philosophy) that aim to mimic the cognitive abilities of humans. Its developments are closely related to those in computer science. They have resulted in computers being able to perform increasingly complex tasks that previously could only be assigned to humans.

However, this automation is still a long way from human intelligence in the strict sense, which has criticized the term among some experts. The final stage of their research (a "strong" AI, i.e., the ability to contextualize very different specialized problems completely autonomously) is not comparable to current achievements ("weak" or "moderate" AI, extremely efficient in its training domain). "Strong" AI, which so far exists only in science fiction, would require advances in basic research (not just performance improvements) to be able to model the world as a whole.

Since 2010, however, the discipline has experienced a resurgence, mainly due to significant improvements in computer processing power and access to vast amounts of data.

Promises, renewed and sometimes fantasized concerns complicate an objective understanding of the phenomenon. Nevertheless, brief historical recollections can help situate the discipline and inform current debates.

1940-1960: The birth of AI

The period between 1940 and 1960 was strongly marked by the combination of technological developments (whose accelerator was World War II) and the desire to understand how to bring together machines and organic beings' workings. For Norbert Wiener, a cybernetics pioneer, the goal was to unite mathematical theory, electronics, and automation as "a whole theory of control and communication, both in animals and machines." Shortly before, the first mathematical and computer model of the biological neuron (formal neuron) had already been developed in 1943 by Warren McCulloch and Walter Pitts.

John Von Neumann and Alan Turing did not create the term AI in early 1950, but they were the founders of the technology behind it: they made the transition from computers to 19th-century decimal logic (which thus dealt with values from 0 to 9) and from machines to binary logic (which is based on Boolean algebra and deals with more or less important chains of 0 or 1). The two researchers thus formalized our computers' architecture today and showed that it is a universal machine capable of executing what is programmed. Turing, on the other hand, in his famous 1950 article "Computing Machinery and Intelligence," first raised the question of the possible intelligence of a machine and described a "game of imitation" in which a human should be able to distinguish in a teletype dialogue whether he is talking to a human or a machine. As controversial as this article may be (the "Turing test" seems out of the question for many experts), it is often cited as a source for questioning the boundary between humans and machines.

The term "AI" could be traced back to John McCarthy of MIT (Massachusetts Institute of Technology), defined by Marvin Minsky (Carnegie-Mellon University) as "the construction of computer programs to perform tasks currently performed more satisfactorily by humans because they require high-level mental processes such as Perceptual learning, memory organization, and critical thinking. The conference in the summer of 1956 at Dartmouth College (funded by the Rockefeller Institute) is the discipline's origin. Anecdotally, this event's great success, which was not a conference but rather a workshop, is worthy of note. Unfortunately, only six people, including McCarthy and Minsky, were consistently present during this work (which was largely based on formal logic developments).

While the technology remained intriguing and promising (see, for example, the 1963 article by Reed C. Lawlor, a California Bar Association member, entitled "What Computers Can Do: Analysis and Prediction of Judicial Decisions"), its popularity declined in the early 1960s. The machines had very little memory, which made it difficult to use a computer language. However, there were some basics already in place that are still around today, such as solution trees for solving problems: For example, IPL, the Information Processing Language, made it possible to write the program LTM (Logic Theorist Machine) as early as 1956 to demonstrate mathematical theorems.

Herbert Simon, economist and sociologist, predicted in 1957 that AI would succeed in beating a human at chess within the next ten years. Simon's vision proved to be correct 30 years later.

1980-1990: Expert systems

In 1968, Stanley Kubrick made the movie "2001 A Space Odyssey," in which a computer - HAL 9000 (just one letter removed from those of IBM) - encapsulates the whole sum of ethical questions raised by AI: Will it represent a high level of sophistication, a good for humanity, or a danger? The film's impact will not be scientific, but it will help popularize the subject, just like science fiction writer Philip K. Dick, who kept wondering if machines would one day feel emotions.

With the advent of the first microprocessors in the late 1970s, AI picked up steam again and entered the expert systems' golden age.

The path was opened in 1965 at MIT with DENDRAL (expert system specialized in molecular chemistry) and in 1972 at Stanford University with MYCIN (system specialized in diagnosing blood diseases and prescription drugs). These systems were based on an "inference machine" programmed to be a logical mirror of human thought. By inputting data, the machine provided answers at a high technical level.

The promises foresaw a massive development, but the delusion fell again in late 1980 and early 1990. Programming such knowledge was very costly, and from 200 to 300 rules, there was a "black box" effect where it was unclear how the machine reasoned; This made development and maintenance extraordinarily problematic and, more importantly, faster and possible in many other less complicated and less expensive ways. It is worth remembering that in the 1990s, artificial intelligence was almost taboo, and more modest variants, such as "advanced computing," had even entered university parlance.

Deep Blue's success (IBM's expert system) in the May 1997 chess match against Garry Kasparov fulfilled Herbert Simon's 1957 prophecy 30 years later but did not support the funding and development of this form of AI. Deep Blue's operation was based on a systematic brute force algorithm in which all possible moves were evaluated and weighted. The defeat of man remained very symbolic in history, but

Deep Blue had, in fact, only managed to deal with a minimal scope (that of the rules of chess), very far from being able to model the complexity of the world.

Since 2010: The rise of available data and computing power

Two factors explain the discipline's new boom around 2010.

1. One is access to vast amounts of data. In the past, you had to do your sampling to use algorithms for image classification and cat detection. Today, a simple search on Google is enough to find millions.

2. The discovery of the very high performance of computer graphics card processors to speed up the computation of learning algorithms. Since the process is very iterative, it could take weeks to process the entire sample by 2010. However, these cards' computational power (capable of more than a thousand billion transactions per second) enabled considerable progress at a small financial cost (less than 1000 euros per card).

This new technological equipment has enabled significant public successes and boosted funding: in 2011, Watson, IBM's IA, won the games against 2 Jeopardy champions! ». In 2012,

Google X (Google's search lab) will have an AI recognizing cats on a video. More than 16,000 processors were used for this last task, but the potential is extraordinary: a machine learns to distinguish something. In 2016, AlphaGo (Google's AI specialized in Go games) defeated the European champion (Fan Hui) and then the world champion (Lee Sedol) himself (AlphaGo Zero). Let's keep in mind that Go has much more critical combinatorics than chess (more than the number of particles in the universe) and that it is impossible to achieve such significant results in raw strength (as with Deep Blue in 1997).

Where did this marvel come from? A complete paradigm shift from expert systems. The approach has become inductive: It is no longer a matter of encoding rules as in expert systems but of letting computers discover them by correlation and classification based on a massive amount of data.

Deep Learning seems to be the most promising for various applications (including speech or image recognition). In 2003, Geoffrey Hinton (University of Toronto), Yoshua Bengio (University of Montreal), and Yann LeCun (New York University) decided to launch a research program to bring neural networks up to speed. Experiments conducted simultaneously at Microsoft, Google, and IBM using Hinton's Toronto lab showed that this learning type reduced speech recognition error rates in half. Hinton's team achieved similar results in image recognition.

Overnight, a large majority of research teams turned to this technology, with undeniable benefits. This type of learning has also enabled considerable progress in text recognition, but experts like Yann LeCun say there is still a long way to go before we have systems that understand the text. Conversational agents illustrate this challenge well: our smartphones already know how to transcribe an instruction but cannot fully contextualize it and analyze our intentions.

# THREE ESSAYS FOR THE FUNDAMENTAL UNDERSTANDING OF AI

## Artificial Intelligence: An attempt to define and distinguish

The development of Artificial Intelligence can be seen as the latest wave of automation since industrialization. While in the late 19th and early 20th centuries, the focus of automation was mainly on the substitution of physical human work by machines, artificial intelligence is the attempt to recreate human-like structures of perception and decision-making (to enable machines to perform specific (cognitive) tasks as well as, or even better than, a human being). A clear definition of the term artificial intelligence does not exist until today. AI can be defined as follows:

*"The designing and building of intelligent agents that receive percepts from the environment and take actions that affect that environment."*

(Russell and Norvig 1995)

## Types of AI

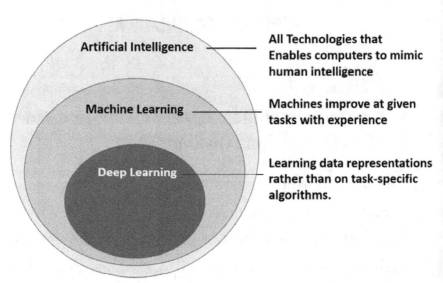

A distinction is made between a strong and weak AI. Weak artificial intelligence (AI) aims to solve concrete, clearly defined application problems; This is done based on mathematical methods (algorithms) especially developed and optimized for the individual requirement. Therefore, weak AI is designed to support people in a specific activity.

These rule-based systems are primarily designed to perform clearly defined tasks without understanding problem-solving. This form of AI is already used in many areas, such as character and image recognition, individual control of advertising, knowledge-based expert systems, and navigation systems.

In contrast, strong artificial intelligence (also known as superintelligence or strong AI or AGI (Artificial General Intelligence)) is characterized by possessing the same intellectual skills as humans or even surpassing them. A strong AI no longer acts reactively but intelligently and flexibly on its initiative. Artificial intelligence should be enabled to generalize and abstract in addition to other cognitive abilities. To date, developing such a strong AI has not yet been possible. It is also not clear whether this will ever be possible to achieve this goal.

The oldest widely used artificial intelligence definition is the so-called Turing test. According to this test, artificial intelligence can be attributed to a machine if a human conversation partner cannot identify whether the other person is a human or a machine. AI systems also vary in terms of complexity and abilities. Simple AI systems are based on fixed codes, based on which they can often solve tasks very quickly and infinitely. An example of this is the chess software Deep Blue from IBM. Deep Blue was the first computer program that could defeat a reigning world chess champion. However, this simple type of AI is limited to areas with clearly defined rules and visual solutions.

The next level of AI systems is so-called machine learning. It is based on the fact that the AI learns from available data and uses it for decisions. A system can optimize and adapt its algorithms based on experience.

Through machine learning, for example, the computer program Watson was able to defeat the human participants at the Jeopardy quiz show (more info). The challenge with Jeopardy! is that answers to primarily ambiguously formulated questions have to be found within a time limit of five seconds. Watson used several types of machine learning, such as rule-based syntax analysis, knowledge bases, and logistic regression, to interpret natural language, evaluate data sources, generate as many answers as possible, and then use statistical methods to select the most likely one. Other significant achievements in this area include AlphaGo and DeepStack.

The most promising discipline of machine learning is artificial neural networks, also called deep learning; This involves analyzing and evaluating vast amounts of data, drawing logical conclusions, and selecting solutions. Systems based on Deep Learning can learn from experience and understand complicated contexts in the world. For example, cancer researchers at the University of California have built an innovative microscope for automatically detecting cancer cells that provide a high-dimensional amount of data that can be used to train a deep learning application to precisely identify cancer cells.

# 5 Variations of Artificial Intelligence

According to an unofficial consensus, the birth of artificial intelligence as an independent research project can be dated to the summer of 1956, when John McCarthy at Dartmouth College, where he belonged to the Mathematical Department, was able to persuade the Rockefeller Foundation to finance an investigation" The study is to proceed on the basis of the conjecture that every aspect of learning or any other feature of intelligence can in principle be so precisely described that a machine can be made to simulate it". In addition to McCarthy (who was a professor at Stanford University until 2000 and is responsible for the coining of the term "artificial intelligence"), several other participants took part in the historical workshop at Dartmouth: Marvin Minsky (former professor at Stanford University), Claude Shannon (inventor of information theory); Herbert Simon (Nobel Prize winner in economics); Arthur Samuel (developer of the first chess computer program at world champion level); furthermore half a dozen experts from science and industry, who dreamed that it might be possible to produce a machine for coping with human tasks, which, according to the previous opinion, require intelligence.

The Manifesto of Dartmouth (written at the dawn of the AI age) is irritating and blurred. It is unclear whether the conference participants believed that machines would think or behave as if they could imagine one day. Both possible interpretations allow the word "simulate." Written and oral reports on the meeting support both positions. Some participants were concerned with studies of networks of artificial neurons, which, they hoped, could, in some sense, recreate the biological neurons of the brain. While others were more interested in producing programs that should behave intelligently, regardless of whether the principles underlying the plans bear any resemblance to the functioning of the human brain. This gap between the paradigms

**Thinking = the way the brain does it,**

**&**

**Thinking = the results that the brain produces.**

The AI community is divided into the so-called strong and weak AI schools.

To better understand what machines can think about, it may be helpful to differentiate the dichotomy "strong" and "weak" a little and compare it with a scheme suggested by the philosopher Keith Gunderson. He distinguishes between the following AI Varieties:

**1. Weak AI, task, non-simulation:** The computer can perform tasks that previously required intelligence, but no intelligence is required of the machine whose states have nothing to do with humans or other cognition.

**2. Weak AI, simulation, non-human:** A computer can simulate the cognitive processes in a non-human brain, but the states of the machine may or may not be related to those in the non-human brain.

**3. Weak AI, simulation, human:** A computer can simulate human cognitive processes, but there is no specific correlation between the computer states and the mental states of the brain

**4. Strong AI, non-human**: The cognitive states found in machines are not functionally identical to those in the brain and, therefore, cannot be used to recreate human thought processes.

**5. Strong AI, human:** The cognitive states of the machines are functional (although not physical by nature) and identical to those found in the human brain.

We must clarify the difference between the functional and physically identical pairs of states. The easiest way to tell the difference is to imagine that we are dealing with a correspondence between the cognitive states C1, C2, C3, and three machine states, M1, M2, and M3. These states are not physically identical because the machine states are merely patterns of the numbers 0 and 1 on a silicon chip. The cognitive states are coupled to the brain's chemical concentrations and electrical patterns. However, the two-state sequences would be functionally equivalent if, for example, we found that the machine pattern M1->M3->M2 corresponds to the cognitive pattern C2->C3->C1 each time. In this case, we could say that the states M3 and C3 are functionally identical because they play the same functional role in the respective sequences; i.e., they are always the three-part series's mean state.

As far as real machine thinking is concerned, the first category in the above overview is the only important one: strong AI, human. Although technically attractive and economically rewarding, everything else lacks any real intellectual or philosophical temptation, at least regarding the question of machines of thought; This may surprise some, given the massive hype that the media (and various self-service representatives of the AI Guild) have recently been organizing. They praise the wonders of the so-called expert systems developed in the AI labs of Massachusetts, London, and Tokyo, enthusiastically describe the robots and programs waiting around the corner to fulfill all our wishes (or take away our jobs), and demand that more money is thrown out of the window. Not to mention the speculation of the capitalists/entrepreneurs and their computer-fixed allies, who are romping about everywhere, trying to capitalize on people's credulity in machines' mindsets. This deplorable situation can be traced back to a handful of programs that demonstrate progress in the last and intellectually not incredibly productive category: weak AI, abandonment, and non-simulation.

Progress in this area says as much about thinking as the flight mechanism of birds about the aircraft's development. So from now on, when we talk about cognitive states in machines, we refer to the types of rules described in our first category: strong AI, human.

Of course, no one has yet put forward an unassailable argument to the effect that the inner states of an appropriately programmed digital computer are functionally identical to the rules of consciousness when they covetously eye a luxury car, examine the seemingly endless menu in a Chinese restaurant, check their account balance, enjoy a Bach fugue, or devote themselves to one of the myriads of other activities that we call thinking in a certain sense.

In the short term, AI will continue to be dominated by point 2. The most recent example is the victory of an expert system against one of the world's best Go players. (Consider the incredibly high number of 2.08 x 10 to the power of 170 different positions on a 19×19 Go board. In comparison, chess has "only "10 to the power of 43 different positions. The number of atoms in the universe is about 10 to the power of 80!). The following years (3-10) will strongly dominate by points 3 and 4. It will come so far that we cannot always say with certainty whether we are dealing with 'real' consciousness or whether it is just a brilliant simulation taking place right in front of us. The progressive development in the field of robotics will do the rest. AI embedded in a quasi-human body will affect us more than text output on a screen or speech from a smartphone device.

# Duplication versus Simulation

There is still much confusion about this point in the AI community. Therefore, with this article, I want to present my view on the relationship between duplication and simulation because it is of great importance that there is clarity here.

The philosopher John Searle has attached great importance to this point by explaining that a simulation is not duplicated. A machine cannot duplicate human thought but simulate it at best. On the fact that simulation and duplication are two pairs of boots, I fully agree with him.

Suppose we have two kinds of objects in front of us, say, an Audi A4 (neither my favorite car nor do I drive it) and a second object that someone claims to be a "duplicate" or a "model" of the Audi A4. What exactly does that mean? What is a model of the A4? It means exactly what a ten-year-old interested in car models understands by it. Namely, there is a direct correspondence between the external stimuli, internal states, and behavior of the A4 and the model's inputs, internal states, and outputs. The correspondence does not necessarily have to be one hundred percent. Thus, some external stimuli, states, and behaviors of Model A4 may not be present in the model. One human brain is not the same as another. If, for example, you go to Ingolstadt (Audi Headquarters) and look at a model of the A4 in the wind tunnel, you will see that the seats, the navigation, etc., may be in the model... and all the other equipment details that make up many of the internal states of the "real" Audi A4 are missing – for the simple reason that they are irrelevant to the purpose of the model, i.e., testing the aerodynamic properties of the right car.

Nevertheless, the model's external stimuli, states, and behaviors are directly related to a subset of the actual engine's inputs, states, and actions. Such correspondence results in a model relationship between the real A4 and the object in the wind tunnel. Note that the model is more straightforward than the actual object it replicates in that it has fewer states. This property is characteristic of model names: Models are always more straightforward than their originals.

What about a simulation?

Let's take a printer of the brand X, whose operating instructions assure me that I can imitate, i.e., simulate, another type of printer, e.g., a HP Laserjet Plus. What does it mean when people say that my X machine can simulate another device?

That means that the HP machine inputs and states can be encoded into my machine's states, and those same states of my machine can then be decoded into the correct outputs that a real HP printer would produce. What is important is that my machine has to be more complicated than the HP in a certain sense if such a dictionary of encryption and decryption is created. To be more precise: To encrypt the inputs and the states of the HP into the states of my simulator, my machine must have more states than the HP printer if you regard both devices as abstract machines. Therefore, the simulator (my printer) must be more complicated than the simulated object (the HP printer). In general, simulation is always more complex than the system it simulates.

These short, perhaps even common, and casual explanations about models and simulations can be translated into exact mathematical terms. Provided, of course, that there are criteria that can be verified in principle. We can use it to distinguish a program that simulates human thought processes in the model from another that merely simulates them. In this context, it is exciting that a brain simulation requires a system with more states than the brain itself. This fact justifiably makes much doubt whether the brain as a whole can ever be simulated.

The brain, with its approximately 100 billion neurons, has at least 2 to the power of 10 to the power of 11 possible states - a number that deserves the highest respect in every respect because it far exceeds even the number of protons in the universe known to us (10 to the power of 79) by a factor of approximately two to the power of 100 billion. Even this number is so large that it is difficult to express it in words. Not to mention his idea. We can, therefore, safely assume that there will be no simulation of the human brain in the medium and long term (the Human Brain Project, funded by the EU, has a similar objective).

Brain models are an entirely different matter, and it is good that the "strong AI, human" needs models and not simulations. But, all in all, I have the impression that the thinking machine debate is a battle between philosophers, not computer scientists and programmers.

My feeling tells me we will have a genuine machine in our house in the next ten to fifteen years. It is based mainly on the fact that we will work out new concepts in connection with new hardware, such as neuromorphic computing, in information processing (To name just one of the upcoming innovations in information processing). Can it then be called "strong AI, human"? That's another interesting question that must be answered in due course. According to what criteria and standards? These questions will have to determine by philosophers, psychologists, and anthropologists.

However, for my part, I can conclude this brief excursion with an unambiguous and definitive statement: Whatever the outcome of the matter of "strong AI, human," the result will radically change our self-image and our view of our position in the cosmic order.

# ARTICLES

## Why we need to Regulate the use of AI Technologies

The potential benefits of AI for our societies are manifold, from improved medical care and knowledge discovery to better and more efficient education. However, given the rapid technological development of AI, we should be especially mindful of this technology because significant risks are not far from where great opportunities open up. While most AI systems pose little to no risk, specific AI systems create risks that must be addressed to avoid undesirable effects on people and society. For example, the opaque nature of many algorithms can generate uncertainty and bias and hinder the effective enforcement of existing security and fundamental rights legislation.

Note:

Although existing legislation provides some protection, it is not sufficient to address the unique challenges that AI systems may pose.

The proposed regulations will:

> ➢ address the risks explicitly posed by AI applications;
> ➢ submit a list of high-risk applications;
> ➢ establish precise requirements for AI systems for high-risk applications;
> ➢ set specific obligations for AI users and providers of high-risk applications;
> ➢ submit a conformity assessment before the AI system is placed in service or on the market;
> ➢ propose enforcement after such an AI system is placed on the market;
> ➢ Propose a governance structure at the European and national levels.

(Based on the recommendations of the European Commision)

Regulatory and legislative measures are needed to address these challenges. This is the only way to ensure a well-functioning market for AI systems where the benefits and risks are adequately addressed. This includes applications such as biometric identification systems, Deep Fakes, or AI decisions that affect critical personal interests, such as recruitment, education, healthcare, or law enforcement. In addition, we need to create a global framework that can ensure the protection of fundamental rights, the safety of all users, and trust in the development and deployment of AI.

Unfortunately, formulating laws alone is not enough. The biggest challenge will be to monitor such systems. It is also essential that AI regulation should always be based on observation and insights. As AI develops dynamically, one should quickly evaluate the latest achievements and adapt legislation accordingly. We must create an internationally organized and operating unit to audit and monitor AI systems worldwide concerning the impact and risks to society. It is questionable whether such an organization can be established nationwide.

*We are still at the beginning. While AI is developing faster and faster, we are lagging behind legislation and regulatory measures. We must catch up quickly if we don't want AI to overtake us one day.*

# Do Companies need a Chief AI-Ethics Officer?

The world we live in is becoming more and more data-driven; This is causing companies to use more and more AI techniques such as machine learning and deep learning. It seems to be the only "efficient" way to get control over the data and generate value for the company relatively quickly. But, of course, future competitiveness also plays a significant role.

The task of the Chief AI Ethics Officer (CAIEO) should not be primarily technical. Instead, it should sensitize data scientists, machine learning engineers, and developers to ethical issues. The whole process of sensitization should be part of every data-driven project. I mean that the ethical workflow should be firmly integrated into the respective process models and phases.

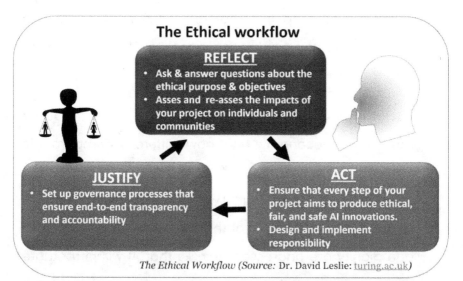

*The Ethical Workflow (Source:* Dr. David Leslie: turing.ac.uk*)*

Source: "Understanding artificial intelligence ethics and safety" by the Alan Turing Institute

In the long term, AI may lead to 'breakthroughs' in numerous fields. From basic and applied science to medicine and advanced systems. However, as well as great promise, increasingly capable intelligent systems create significant ethical challenges. The issues discussed deal with impacts on: human society; human psychology; the financial system; the legal system; the environment and the planet; and impacts on trust.

Below are some points that an AI-Ethics officer should consider in their work (According to EPRS | European Parliamentary Research Service).

**Social impacts:** the potential impact of AI on the labor market and economy and how different demographic groups might be affected. It addresses questions of inequality and the risk that AI will further concentrate power and wealth in the hands of the few. Privacy, human rights, and dignity are addressed as risks that AI will perpetuate the biases, intended or otherwise, of existing social systems or their creators. This section also raises questions about the impact of AI technologies on democracy, suggesting that these technologies may operate for the benefit of state-controlled economies.

**Psychological impacts:** what impacts might arise from human-robot relationships? How might we address dependency and deception? Should we consider whether robots deserve to be given the status of 'personhood', and what are the legal and moral implications of doing so?

**Financial system impacts:** potential impacts of AI on economic systems are considered, including risks of manipulation and collusion and the need to build in accountability.

**Legal system impacts:** there are several ways in which AI could affect the legal system, including questions relating to crime, such as liability if an AI is used for criminal activities and the extent to which AI might support criminal activities such as drug trafficking. In situations where an AI is involved in personal injuries, such as in a collision involving an autonomous vehicle, questions arise around the legal approach to claims (whether it is a case of negligence, which is usually the basis for allegations involving vehicular accidents or product liability).

**Environmental impacts:** increasing use of AIs come with increased use of natural resources, increased energy demands, and waste disposal issues. However, AIs could improve how we manage waste and resources, leading to environmental benefits.

**Impacts on trust:** society relies on trust. For AI to take on tasks like surgery, the public will need to trust the technology. Trust includes aspects such as fairness (that AI will be impartial), transparency (that we will be able to understand how an AI arrived at a particular decision), accountability (someone can be held accountable for mistakes made by AI) and control (how we might 'shut down' an AI that becomes too powerful).

It is primarily about identifying & understanding ethical risks and training managers & employees on how to do the same.

Chief AI-Ethics Officer: The Job of the Future?

Discussions about AI Ethics are still primarily conducted in academic circles. But one can already see that many companies are earnestly dealing with it. One thing that seems clear to me:

*Graduates of philosophy and ethics will be in high demand in the future to investigate AI-related processes through a human lens.*

# Employment and Skills in the Age of AI

Some thoughts about the facets of employment in the future:

> ***The fear of job loss through AI is omnipresent and justified, but it also has a positive aspect. We are forced to think more seriously about redefining work. And That's a good thing***

There is no doubt that we are currently in the transition phase into the Age of AI. The dynamics of the whole thing are getting faster every day. We must not fall into the belief of thinking: This will all take some time, and we have enough time to think about the influences of AI on us humans and society. Nowadays, nobody can estimate the developments in the field of AI accurately. The best way to see this is that even the so-called Experts have different opinions.

> ***The use of Artificial Intelligence is a superior form of delegating tasks; without loss of control!***

In my opinion, the future type of employment in the Age of AI can be roughly categorized into two areas:

**1. AI-Enabling**

**2. AI-Supervising/Evaluating.**

**AI-Enabling**

A lot is already happening in this area. For example, more and more IoT devices are coming onto the market, and machines that are not yet able to produce data or have interfaces are being retrofitted.

Looking at the job market in recent years, you can see that more and more data scientists, ML/Data-Engineers, and AI Experts are being sought. As a result, almost every university offers AI courses/degrees. There are even pure AI-Universities where everything is designed around AI.

There is also a lot going on in hardware development and technology advancement. New approaches like neuromorphic chips and quantum computing are becoming more and more mature.

Due to the ever-increasing focus on AI, the community and the number of "Experts" are increasing. As a result, algorithms/network topologies are continuously improved and optimized.

**Biggest challenges:**

➢ Making algorithms more efficient, -transparent, -explainable, and -fair
➢ Standards
➢ Security
➢ Robustness
➢ AI-Supervising/Evaluating

Here it does not look so good yet, but we slowly realize AI's significant influence on our lives and society. As a result, humans have to reposition themselves and rethink their way of thinking in some areas.

It will not be easy, so we will need more philosophers, sociologists, and psychologists to help us deal with all these changes and use them to our advantage.

We need to become more real thinkers, not to say, philosophers. Soft skills like Growth Mindset, Creativity, Emotional Intelligence, Culture Awareness, and Focus Mastery become "vital qualities" because the monotonous and rule-based will ideally no longer exist for us humans.

Even Professor John McCarthy recognized the importance of philosophy even then. But unfortunately, we often get lost in the technical details and neglect the holistic view of the subject area. The sum is more different than its parts.

**Biggest challenge:**

We must change / adapt our mindset.

*Artificial intelligence must be oriented towards humans and should have merely a complementary function.*

*We are in the midst of a transition period. The more advanced Artificial Intelligence becomes, the more uncertainty spreads. We must reposition ourselves and change our mindset if we don't want to perish.*

# The Criminal Potential of Artificial Intelligence

I omitted this article to denigrate AI or to stir up fears (I believe AI will bring more benefits to humanity than any other technology to date) but to point out the dangers AI can pose and how it can be abused.

AI can be implicated in crime in several ways. Most obviously, AI could be used as a tool for crime, using its capabilities to facilitate actions against real-world targets: predicting the behavior of people or institutions to discover and exploit vulnerabilities; generating fake content for extortion or to damage reputations; performing acts that human perpetrators cannot or will not perform themselves for reasons of danger, physical size, speed of response, etc. Although the methods are new, the crimes themselves may be traditional in nature - theft, extortion, intimidation, terror.

Alternatively, AI systems themselves may be the target of criminal activity: Circumventing protective systems that stand in the way of a crime; evading detection or prosecution of crimes already committed; causing trusted or critical systems to fail or misbehave cause harm or undermine public trust.

AI could also provide context for a crime. The fraudulent activity could depend on the victim believing that a certain AI functionality is possible when it is not - or that it is possible but not used for the fraud.

Of course, these categories are not mutually exclusive. As in the adage about catching a thief, an AI system attack may itself require an AI system to be carried out. The fraudulent simulation of nonexistent AI capabilities could be executed using other AI methods that exist.

Crimes vary enormously. They may be directed against individuals or institutions, businesses or customers, property, government, the social fabric, or public discourse. They may be motivated by financial gain, acquisition of power, or change in status relative to others. They may enhance or damage reputations or relationships, change policy, or sow discord; such effects may be an end in themselves or a stepping stone to a broader goal. They may be committed to mitigate or avoid punishment for other crimes. They may be driven by a desire for revenge or sexual gratification or to further religious or political goals. They may express nothing more than a nihilistic urge to destroy, vandalize, or commit violence for its own sake.

The extent to which AI can amplify this variety of criminal acts depends mostly on how much they are embedded in a computational environment: Robotics is advancing rapidly, but AI is better suited to participate in a bank fraud than in a bar fight. This preference for the digital over the physical world is a weak defense. However, because today's society is deeply dependent on complex computer networks, not only for finance and commerce but also for all forms of communication, politics, news, work, and social relationships. People now conduct large parts of their lives online, get most of their information there, and their online activities can make or break their reputations. This trend is likely to continue for the foreseeable future. Such an online environment, where data is property and information power, is ideally suited for exploitation by AI-based criminal activities that can have significant real-world consequences. Moreover, unlike many traditional crimes, crimes in the digital domain are often highly reproducible: once developed, techniques can be shared, repeated, and even sold, opening up the potential for commercializing criminal techniques or providing "crime as a service." This can lead to a lowering of technological barriers as criminals are able to outsource the more challenging aspects of their AI-based crimes.

Listed below are some potential hazards.

## Audio and video imitation

People have a strong tendency to believe their own eyes and ears, so audio and video evidence has traditionally been given a lot of credibilities (and often legal force), despite the long history of photo trickery. But recent developments in Deep Learning, mainly using GANs (see above), have greatly expanded the scope for generating fake content. Persuasive impersonations of targets following a fixed script can already be produced, and interactive impersonations are expected to follow. Delegates saw multiple criminal applications for such "deepfake" technologies to exploit people's implicit trust in these media, including Impersonation of children to elderly parents via video calls to gain access to funds; use over the phone to gain access to secure systems, and fake videos of public figures speaking or acting reprehensibly to manipulate support. Audio/video impersonation was ranked as the most concerning type of crime overall of all those considered, scoring high on all four dimensions. Combating it was considered difficult: Researchers have shown some success with algorithmic detection of Impersonation, but this may not be possible in the longer term, and there are very many uncontrolled pathways through which fake material can spread. Changes in citizen behavior may therefore be the only effective defense. These behavioral changes, such as a general distrust of visual evidence, could be considered indirect societal harms resulting from the crime, in addition to direct harms such as fraud or damage to reputation. If even a small fraction of visual evidence turns out to be convincing fakes, it becomes much easier to discredit genuine evidence, undermining criminal investigations and the credibility of political and social institutions that rely on trustworthy communication. Such tendencies are already evident in the discourse around "fake news." Profit has been ranked as the least high dimension for this crime, not because the investment required is high (it is not), but because copycat crimes aimed at acquisition are likely to be most easily targeted against individuals rather than institutions, while copycat crimes against society have an uncertain impact.

**Driverless vehicles as weapons**

Motor vehicles have long been used both as a means of transporting explosives and as stand-alone kinetic terrorist weapons, with the latter becoming increasingly common in recent years. Vehicles are much more readily available than firearms and explosives in most countries, and attacks using vehicles can be carried out with relatively little organizational effort by fragmented, quasi-autonomous, or "lone wolf" terrorists. While fully autonomous, AI-driven driverless vehicles are not yet available, numerous automakers and technology companies work diligently to develop them, with some trials permitted on public roads. More limited self-driving capabilities, such as assisted parking and lane guidance, are already in use. Autonomous vehicles would potentially enable an expansion of vehicular terrorism by reducing the need to recruit drivers and allowing lone wolves to carry out multiple attacks and even coordinate a large number of vehicles at once. Because driverless cars will almost certainly have extensive security systems that would need to be overridden, driverless attacks will have a higher entry barrier than they currently do because they require technological capability and organization.

## Tailored phishing

Phishing is a "social engineering" attack that aims to collect secure information or install malware via a digital message that purports to come from a trusted party such as the user's bank. The attacker exploits the existing trust to get the user to perform actions they would otherwise shy away from, such as revealing passwords or clicking on dubious links. Some attacks may target specific individuals, which is known as "spear phishing," but this is not very scalable. Currently, most phishing attacks are relatively indiscriminate, using generic messages crafted after major brands or current events that can be expected to be of interest to a subset of users purely by chance. The attacker relies on the ease of sending a large number of digital messages to turn a low response rate into a profitable return. AI has the potential to improve phishing attack success rates by creating messages that appear more genuine by (for example) including information from social networks or faking the style of a trusted party. Rather than sending uniform messages to all targets, which in most cases miss their target, messages could instead be tailored to exploit the specific vulnerabilities inferred for each individual, effectively automating the spear-phishing approach. Additionally, AI methods could use active learning to figure out "what works" by varying the details of the messages to gather data on how to maximize responses.

## Disruption of AI-controlled systems

As AI's use in government, business, and the private sector increases and the tasks performed by AI systems become more important, the opportunities for attacks will also increase. Learning systems are often deployed for efficiency and convenience rather than robustness and may not be recognized as critical infrastructure in the first place. Delegates were able to envision many criminal and terrorist scenarios resulting from targeted disruption of such systems, from causing widespread power outages to gridlock and the collapse of food logistics. Systems responsible for all aspects of public safety are likely to become prime targets, as are those that monitor financial transactions.

## Large scale blackmail

Traditional extortion involves extortion under threat of disclosure of evidence of criminal or wrongful conduct or embarrassing personal information. A limiting factor in traditional extortion is obtaining such evidence: The crime is only worthwhile if the victim pays more to suppress the evidence than it costs to obtain it. AI can be used to do this on a much larger scale, gathering information (which need not itself be incriminating evidence) from social media or large personal data sets such as email logs, browser histories, hard drive or phone content, then identifying specific vulnerabilities for a large number of potential targets and tailoring threatening messages to each. AI could also be used to generate fake evidence, such as when the discovered information implies a vulnerability without providing prima facie evidence).

## AI-created Fake News

Fake news is propaganda that aims to gain credibility by coming from or appearing to come from a trusted source. Fake News not only provides false information but in sufficient quantity can divert attention from real information. AI could be used to generate many versions of a given piece of content, seemingly from multiple sources, to increase its visibility and credibility and to select the content or its presentation on a personalized basis to increase its impact.

## Military robots

As in many areas of technological development, the military has a significant interest in robotics research, with potentially very different goals than civilian users, despite many methodological overlaps. Any availability of military hardware (e.g., firearms or explosives) to criminal or terrorist organizations is likely to pose a serious threat, and this would certainly be the case for autonomous robots intended for the battlefield or defensive use.

## Snake oil

Selling fraudulent services under the guise of AI or under the guise of ML jargon. Such a scam is extremely easy to pull off as there is almost no technical barrier (as the technology, by definition, does not work). The potential profits are high: there are many infamous historical examples of fraudsters selling expensive technological gimmicks to large organizations, including national governments and the military. This is arguably not the use of AI for crime, but the crime depends on the target's belief in the claimed AI capabilities, which depends on AI being perceived as successful by the public. It should be potentially easy to defeat through education and due diligence.

## Data poisoning

Manipulating ML training data to intentionally introduce certain biases, either as an end in itself (with the goal of harming commercial competitors, distorting political discourse, or sowing public distrust) or with the intent of later exploitation. For example, by making an automated X-ray threat detector insensitive to weapons you want to smuggle aboard an airplane, or by getting an investment advisor to make unexpected recommendations that change the market value in ways you have prior knowledge of and can exploit. The more widespread and trusted the data source, the more damaging this could be.

## Learning-based cyber attacks

Existing cyberattacks are either sophisticated and tailored to a specific target or crude but highly automated and rely on a sheer mass of numbers (e.g., distributed denial-of-service attacks, port scanning). AI opens up the possibility of attacks that are both specific and massive, using approaches from reinforcement learning, for example, to probe the vulnerabilities of many systems in parallel before launching multiple attacks simultaneously.

**Autonomous attack drones**

Non-autonomous, radio-controlled drones are already being used for crimes such as smuggling drugs into prisons and have also been responsible for major transportation disruptions. Autonomous drones under onboard AI control potentially enable greater coordination and complexity of attacks and free the perpetrator from the need to be within the transmission range of the drone, making neutralization and apprehension more difficult. Currently, drones are not typically used for violent crime, but their mass and kinetic energy are potentially dangerous when targeted (e.g., in aircraft engines), and they could also be equipped with weapons. Drones could be particularly threatening when operating en masse in self-organizing swarms.

## Online distribution

The primacy of online activities in modern life, in terms of finances, employment, social activities, and citizenship presents a novel target for attacks on the individual: Denial of access to services that have become indispensable is potentially crippling. This could be used as an extortion threat to harm or disenfranchise groups of users or to cause chaos. Some existing phishing and cyberattacks attempt something similar using means such as "ransomware," and quasi-organized groups of human actors sometimes carry out activities such as mass misreporting of abuse on social media, but AI could enable attacks that are both more subtle - carefully tailoring fake activity to violate terms of service and identifying specific points of vulnerability for each individual - and more scalable.

## Fool face recognition

AI systems that perform facial recognition are increasingly being used to prove identity on devices such as smartphones and are also being tested by police and security services for tasks such as tracking suspects in public spaces and speeding up passenger checks at international borders. These systems could be an attractive target for criminals. Some successful attacks have already been demonstrated, including "morphing" attacks that allow a single photographic ID, such as a passport, to pass as (and be used by) multiple people.

**Market Bombing**

Manipulating financial or stock markets through targeted, likely high-frequency trading patterns to harm competitors, currencies, or the economic system as a whole (rather than to profit directly from trading, although that could be a side effect as well) has been discussed. The idea is an AI-powered version of the fictional Cold War Kholstomer plot, which involved a Russian attempt to cause a financial crash by suddenly selling huge holdings of U.S. currency through front companies. Reinforcement learning has been proposed as a method for discovering effective trading strategies, possibly in conjunction with NLP-based media analysis and fake content generation.

**Exploitation of bias**

Discovering and exploiting (existing) learned biases in widely used or influential algorithms. For example, influencing YouTube recommendations to bias viewers towards propaganda or Google rankings boosts products or denigrates competitors. In practice, such behavior is already widespread, often not illegal (although it may violate the provider's terms of service), and even considered (in the form of search engine optimization or SEO) a legitimate (if shady) online business model.

## Burglar bots

Small autonomous robots could enter buildings through small access points such as mailboxes or cat flaps to retrieve keys or open doors to allow human intruders to enter. The technical requirements are very limited, which should make these more feasible than more ambitious classes of autonomous robots.

## Escape AI detection

Police and security agencies are expected to increasingly rely on AI-based triage and automation to manage the ever-growing volumes of data collected during investigations. Attacks that subvert these processes to erase evidence or otherwise thwart detection are likely to become increasingly attractive to criminals. Attacking disruptions (e.g., to hide pornographic material from automatic detection) offers one possible way to do this, although the system knowledge requirements can be prohibitive.

## AI-created fake reviews

Automatically generating content for websites such as Amazon or TripAdvisor to create a false impression of a product or service and lure customers either to or away from that product or service. Such fakery is already being done by human agents. AI could increase efficiency, but the gains and damages from this type's campaign are likely to remain small and localized.

## AI-assisted stalking

Using learning systems to monitor a person's location and activities via social media or personal device data. It also applies to other crimes around coercive relationships, domestic violence, gaslighting, etc. It relates to a recent news story about Western tech companies' complicity in providing apps to enforce social norms in repressive societies.

## Forgery

Creation of counterfeit content, such as art or music, which can be sold under false pretenses about its authorship. This was ranked as the least worrisome threat of all those considered, both in terms of harm and likelihood of success. The capabilities of artificial intelligence are very limited here: It has been possible to create digital images that largely mimic the visual style of great painters, but that is very different from creating actual physical objects that would hold up in a gallery or auction house. The art world has struggled with forgeries for centuries and has extensive (if not always adequate) safeguards in place. AI does not even attempt to overcome most of these obstacles.[3]

---

[3] The findings from this chapter are based on the paper "AI-enabled future crime."Caldwell, M., Andrews, J.T.A., Tanay, T. et al. AI-enabled future crime. Crime Sci 9, 14 (2020). https://doi.org/10.1186/s40163-020-00123-8

# How does machine learning work?

Machine learning is currently the most successful way to breathe some 'intelligence' into computers. The other two types are first the algorithm, where, as in a cooking recipe, all the steps to be done are precisely given to the machine. However, since very few tasks in our world are strictly algorithmic, this method is only used in exceptional cases, such as the pocket calculator.

The second possibility would be to model a small part of our knowledge on the computer; This is also referred to as expert systems, which often work with if-then rules. Intelligent assistants can serve as an example. Specific keywords, such as "book a flight," can query the user with a certain degree of flexibility through various dialog modules regarding when and where they would like to fly. The modeling of knowledge is very complex. Therefore, the functional scope of expert systems is limited. Their advantage lies in the traceability of the system behavior.

Machine learning takes a third approach. Here, it is left to mathematical-statistical methods to "learn" patterns or derive actions from large amounts of data. For example, a system is given 1,000 images of cats and 1,000 photos of dogs with the corresponding designation as a target.

New images can then be automatically classified as cat or dog. In doing so, one has little control over which of the engineer-specified data features are used for learning, such as color or size ratios. Therefore, one should use training data that is as balanced and comprehensive as possible and similar to the data that will be classified later. For example, if one shows the described system a picture of a muffin, it will probably classify it as a dog, the best match. The system does not know features such as feathers or whiskers. It performs pure statistical pattern recognition on the pixels of the images. However, this makes these systems flexible and relatively easy to generate. The disadvantage is the poor traceability of the results and, consequently, the lack of performance guarantees.

Different types of machine learning differ, e.g., whether humans' training data must be excellent or not, whether a system learns permanently based on human evaluation of the results, or whether there is an automatic test.

# Can AI have a consciousness?

Whether AI can develop a consciousness cannot be answered unequivocally. First, it must be clarified what is meant by "consciousness" in the first place. Different properties are associated with this term. A simple form is when organisms not only react to external stimuli but experience them as an internal phenomenon. Animals with differentiated brains have this kind of consciousness. A higher level of consciousness is present when living beings develop thoughts, goals, and interests. Finally, living beings - humans, probably primates, and other highly evolved animals - are "self-aware," perceiving themselves as existing and as individuals.

Philosophical dualism assumes that consciousness cannot be derived from physical processes but is of a fundamentally different - mental - quality. Materialistic positions believe that consciousness is a brain function and that neurological processes correlate with consciousness. Empirical facts support this, e.g., When parts of the brain are not functioning, this leads to changes in consciousness. The human brain consists of 100 billion highly interconnected neurons. One hypothesis is that consciousness emerges as soon as this neuronal networking reaches a high level of complexity so that external stimuli are processed, and brain-internal signals are processed; This has far-reaching consequences for AI. Artificial neural networks (ANN, adaptive computer programs that simulate natural neural networks) are used there. If ANN is sufficiently complex, then, following this hypothesis, artificial consciousness could emerge. Just as neuroscience assumes that consciousness is a brain function, AI research assumes that artificial consciousness arises due to complex ANN.

Whether this is true is currently an open question. ANNs are still far from reaching the necessary complexity. In addition, there are theoretical objections that point out that there is a difference between "having" consciousness (like humans) and only "simulating" consciousness (like ANN/AI). What is exciting is the question of what depth artificial consciousness might develop. Will AI even create its interests at some point?

# What is Singularity?

A "technological singularity" is the point in time when AI is more powerful than human intelligence. Unfortunately, such a "superintelligence" does not yet exist, and there is no indication that it could be developed soon.

"Singularity" and "Artificial Superintelligence" belong to technological utopias rather than actual science and research. They refer to a distant future. Despite their utopian-visionary character, it cannot be ruled out in principle that such a superintelligence will be developed at some point in the future and that a singularity will thus occur.

Although a technological singularity is unreal, it is still a topic of current discussions. Some voices warn of dangers for humanity: AI that is superior to humans turns against them, subjugates them, or even exterminates them. For example, because of faulty programming that sees humans as inferior or because AI is developing its interests and is "consciously" turning against humanity to take over the entire world.

However, current AI research is far from the development of superintelligence. True, the power of AI today is already awe-inspiring: Watson, DeepBlue, and AlphaGo show what AI can do. However, their intelligence is still very specialized: intelligent software plays chess or Go very well, excels at Jeopardy!, recognizes language, or identifies faces. But it is always specialized AI, confined to narrow fields of application. No intelligent software can do everything at once, but humans can. They have a general intelligence of high capability. There is no such thing as "general AI." And according to scientists, AI research is miles away from it. If it could develop a general AI, it would still not be a superintelligence that is better than humans. So, a superintelligence, with it the occurrence of a singularity, is a long way off. From today's perspective, they are more science fiction than science.

# 5 Algorithms that Changed the World

An algorithm is a straightforward rule of action to solve a problem or a class of problems. Algorithms consist of a finite number of well-defined individual steps. Thus, they can be implemented in a computer program for execution and formulated in human language. When solving a problem, a specific input is converted into a particular output.

In the following, five algorithms are listed that have significantly influenced our world.

## 1. Metropolis Algorithm for Monte Carlo

The Metropolis algorithm is a Markov-Chain-Monte-Carlo method for generating states of a system according to the Boltzmann distribution. The more general Metropolis-Hastings algorithm derived from this algorithm makes it possible to simulate sequences of random variables, more precisely Markov chains, which have the desired distribution as stationary distribution, especially in many cases where the distributions of the random variables cannot be simulated directly.

## 2. Simplex Method for Linear Programming

A simplex method (also known as a simplex algorithm) is a numerical optimization method for solving linear optimization problems, also known as linear programs (LP). It solves such a problem exactly after finitely many steps or determines its insolubility or unboundedness. George Dantzig introduced the basic idea of simplex methods in 1947; since then, they have developed into the most critical solution methods of linear optimization in practice through numerous improvements. Simplex methods are pivot methods.

## 3. Fast Fourier Transform

The fast Fourier transform (FFT) is an algorithm for the efficient calculation of discrete Fourier transform (DFT). It can be used to decompose a digital signal into its frequency components, which can then be analyzed. Analogously there is the inverse fast Fourier transformation (IFFT) for the discrete inverse Fourier transformation. The IFFT uses the same algorithms but with conjugated coefficients.

The FFT has numerous applications in engineering, natural sciences, and applied mathematics. It is also used in mobile technologies such as UMTS and LTE and wireless data transmission such as WLAN.

## 4. Quicksort Algorithm for Sorting

Quicksort s a fast, recursive, non-stable sorting algorithm that works on the principle of parts and dominance. It was developed around 1960 by C. Antony R. Hoare in its basic form and has since been improved by many researchers. The algorithm has the advantage of a very short inner loop (which significantly increases the execution speed). It does not require additional memory (apart from the extra space needed on the call stack for recursion).

## 5. QR Algorithm for Computing Eigenvalues

The QR algorithm is a numerical method for calculating all eigenvalues and possibly the eigenvectors of a quadratic matrix. The QR method or QR iteration is based on QR decomposition and was introduced independently by John G. F. Francis and Wera Nikolajewna Kublanowskaja in 1961–1962. A predecessor was the LR algorithm by Heinz Rutishauser (1958), which is less stable and based on LR decomposition. Often the iterates from the QR algorithm converge against the Schur form of the matrix. Therefore, the original procedure is quite complex — even on today's computers — not practicable for matrices with hundreds of thousands of rows and columns.

Derived variants like the multishift method of Z. Bai and James Demmel 1989 and the numerically more stable variant of K. Braman, R. Byers, and R. Mathias 2002 have practical runtimes cubic in the size matrix. The latter method is implemented in the numerical software library LAPACK, which is used in many computer algebra systems (CAS) for the numerical matrix algorithms.

*If I had to pick one, my favorite would be Fast Fourier Transform (FFT), because FFT has numerous applications in engineering, natural sciences, and applied mathematics and has an inherent beauty.*

*~ Murat Durmus*

# EPILOG

## We are not all in the same boat,

## but we all live in the same Data Ocean.

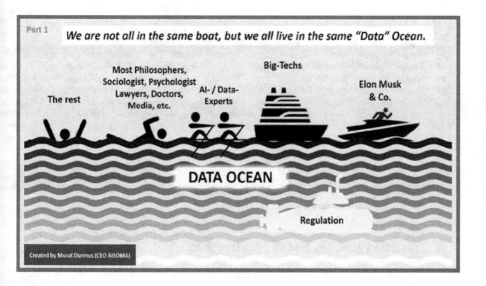

# What we know is a drop,

# what we don't know is an ocean.

## The Story behind these two images

We have access to more knowledge, yet we are becoming more and more "bad thinkers." All the knowledge available should make us smarter, but the opposite is the case. We tend to think fundamentally and all too often forget what matters.

A few people sit on the speedboat and luxury yachts, giving us direction and speed. On the other hand, most of us try to keep up and are exposed to the danger of drowning in information or going blind from it. Technological progress is unstoppable, but ethical, psychological, and sociological aspects are far too short and mostly seen as annoying appendages. Faster, higher, and further until one day, we reach the -Island of Awareness- and realize that we were much too narrow-minded, self-centered, and dogmatic on the way there.

It's about future generations and nature. We must do everything we can to leave them a world worth living in.

Following a short story about "I know that I know nothing":

When Plato's teacher Socrates lived in Athens, his childhood friend Chairephon went to Delphi to ask the Oracle who might be the wisest man in Athens. The Oracle called Socrates, and when he heard of it, he was shocked, and astonished because he did not think he was the smartest. But the God of the Oracle was not allowed to lie, so Socrates wanted to discover what the Oracle might have meant by his saying.

Socrates sought out those who appeared as great teachers and were therefore considered wise in Athens. He wanted to learn from them and thus show that he could not be the wisest because he knew less than the people he addressed. But again and again, he had to find out that Athens' wise teachers became insecure when questioned in detail. He finally had to admit to seeing their knowledge disappear through Socrates' thirst for knowledge. This procedure brought him little sympathy; he was sentenced to death by poison at over 70. He accepted the sentence and said goodbye to his friends with the words: "Now is the time to go, I to die and you to live. But which of us goes to the better business is hidden from all except God."

But back to the Oracle's saying. Through the many discussions with supposedly wise people, Socrates had concluded that neither he nor the others were truly wise. He could now interpret the Oracle saying: "So I seem to be wiser than him in this way because what I don't know, I don't know either."

"I know that I know nothing!" In this abbreviated form, the saying of Socrates is handed down. The aim of Socratic questioning is wisdom, and insight into the limits of knowledge. Knowledge itself does not seem essential. But anyone who wants to experience the boundaries of education cannot avoid the occupation of knowledge. In this indirect way, knowledge also comes into play as a by-product. Anyone who, like Socrates, wants to reach wisdom by accepting not being able to know will also increase his knowledge. He who strives directly for understanding will not attain wisdom with it.

*Note:*

*Goethe presented these two fundamental attitudes in his drama through Heinrich Faust and his Famulus Wagner. While Faust - entirely in the Socratic sense - calls out desperately:*

**"And see that we can't know anything, it almost burns my heart," Wagner soberly says: "I know a lot, but I want to know everything."**

🌀🌀🌀

**I think, therefore, I know that I know nothing.**

# SOME SIGNIFICANT ACHIEVEMENTS IN THE FIELD OF AI SINCE 2010

# 2010

### DeepMind Technologies is founded

A British AI company acquired by Google in 2014 and is part of Alphabet Inc. DeepMind Technologies' most amazing products are the Neural Turing Machine, AlphaFold, Wavenet and WaveRNN, and AlphaGO. In 2014, DeepMind received the "Company of the Year" award from Cambridge Computer Laboratory.

### IBM's Watson computer beats human champions on game show Jeopardy

Watson is an interrogative computer system capable of answering questions posed in natural language. It was developed as part of IBM's DeepQA project by a research team led by study director David Ferrucci. Watson was named after IBM's founder and first CEO, industrialist Thomas J. Watson. The computer system was originally developed to answer questions on the quiz show Jeopardy! In 2011, the Watson computer system competed against champions Brad Rutter and Ken Jennings on Jeardy! and won the first prize of $1 million.

# 2011

## The Google Brain Project

The project was first launched in 2011 as a part-time research project by Google employees Jeff Dean, Greg Corrado, and Stanford University professor Andrew Ng. The project first received significant attention in June 2012, when a computer cluster of 16 thousand computers designed to replicate the human brain early recognized a cat based on YouTube images.

## Apple introduced SIRI on the iPhone 4s

Apple launched SIRI as the first speech assistance program with the iPhone 4S. Speech Interpretation and Recognition

Interface (SIRI) uses voice commands to perform specific user tasks. These voice commands include calling a person, setting the alarm, sending an email, opening text messages, answering questions, asking for recommendations, and using multiple.

## IBM simulates the human brain up to 4.5 percent

IBM simulates the human brain with the Blue Gene supercomputer. The human brain is a vast network of neurons and synapses at their edges. The human brain has 20 billion neurons with more than 200 trillion synapses. An enormous amount of computing power is required to simulate the entire human brain.

# 2012

## Deep neural networks in image classification

Researchers trained DNNs and introduced deep neural networks in image classification with a significant image database such as ImageNet and outperformed human capabilities in recognizing objects or faces.

## Spaun- The First Computer Model to Generate Complex Behavior

Spaun- The First Computer Model To Produce Complex Behavior was developed by the University of Waterloo, Canada. Their engineers created a model that could lead to human performance on simple tasks. It was modeled with the human brain to function biologically in a realistic way. The Nengo platform was used to operate it.

## A robotic arm of the BrainGate system controlled by the minds of paralyzed patients

In 2012, the BrainGate system's robotic arm was the most advanced innovation in the robotics industry. Paralyzed patients had a 4-millimeter-wide chip implanted in their heads. With it, they could control and command the robotic arm. The computer used in this system decodes neural signals in real-time.

## AI recognized cat from completely unsupervised and unassigned image data

Jeff Dean and Andrew Ng of Google set up a neural network of 16000 personal computers. All these processors were given 10 million unlabeled images as a training set from screenshots of Youtube videos. After running the neural network algorithms, the AI recognized the cat from the image without knowing it was a cat image. This was a major milestone in AI and machine learning history that a machine can recognize completely untrained data images.

## Google releases Google Now, a Google search function

Google Now is a search function for Android and iOS. It provided users with predicted information in the form of information cards based on their search and preference data. It used data from users based on their habits and environment, such as location, browsing history, contacts, etc. Google gradually discontinued it, but its features are still available in Google Search.

# 2013

## Google launches Quantum Artificial Intelligence Lab

Running machine learning algorithms is a complex and computationally intensive task. Conventional computers are not suited for such a load. This is where quantum computers are needed. NASA partnered with Google and the Universities Space Research Association to establish the Quantum Artificial Intelligence Lab for advanced and deep computing. The Quantum AI Lab uses quantum computers from D-Waves Systems.

## The world's first talking robot astronaut, Kirobo

It was developed by the University of Tokyo, Toyota, and the Dentsu company. The talking robot was waiting for the arrival of astronaut Koichi Wakata. Kirobo showed emotion when it met Wakata, giving researchers the insight that machines can also be presented with emotions. Moreover, devices can also provide emotional support to people suffering from loneliness or stress.

## The HRP-2 robot built by Schaft won the DARPA robotics competition

Schaft Inc, a Japanese Google subsidiary, built an HRP-2 robot for DARPA's Robotics Challenge Trials held in Miami. Sixteen teams entered their robots in the competition for eight different tasks critical to disaster relief. These tasks included driving a vehicle, walking across an uneven waste surface, climbing a ladder, clearing a path of debris, passing through doors of different sizes, creating a way through a wall by cutting, closing valves, and connecting a hose.

# 2014

### TrueNorth: the first neuromorphic integrated circuit

TrueNorth, IBM & SyNAPSE prepared the first neuromorphic integrated circuit that received one million individually programmable neurons. They also had 256 individually programmable synapses. Synapse is connected to neurons of the real brain, and the human brain has more than 200 trillion synapses. In TrueNorth, the artificial neurons are emulated with a linear-integrate-and-fire (LLIF) model

## The first robot Pepper made by Softbank for customer service

Softbank prepared a robot, namely the first robot Pepper, to support customer service and relieve humans' burden. The robot was integrated with an emotion engine to interact with customers. Owning Pepper requires $14,000.

## Amazon launches its first AI-mediated virtual assistant, Alexa

Alexa was first used in Amazon Echo smart speakers. It is a fantastic program that can interact with voice commands. It can also be used as a personal assistant to play/stop music, tell the weather forecast, and set the alarm clock. This virtual assistant can also be used for home automation.

# 2015

## NueroRobotics – A Human Brain Project

The NueroRobotics system was closely associated with the human brain model. It interfered with the human brain to loop cognitive experiments in simulated environments closely.

## The First Digital Reconstruction Project of the Somatosensory Cortex

The microcircuitry of the somatosensory cortex of the juvenile rat was done first time digitally. This Digital Reconstruction Project was a combined effort of the Blue Brain Project & the Human Brain Project. It was based on the detailed study of cortical dynamics, in-vitro reproduction, and in-vivo experimental results.

## OpenAI Launched By Elon Musk

OpenAI is an artificial intelligence research and development company aiming to help collaboration between scientists and industry for helpful AI product making. Initially, $1 billion was pledged for a startup. It is thought to be a competitor of DeepMind by Google

# . 2016

## OpenAI releases the OpenAI Gym for reinforcement learning

The OpenAI Gym is a platform that allows you to create programs that attempt to play a variety of video game-like tasks. This is often used in reinforcement learning in artificial intelligence (AI). This platform is used to develop and compare reinforcement learning algorithms. It helps AI agents learn any move that occurs in any games like Pong and Atari. Gym can be used with Python only in Linux or Unix environments.

## AlphaGo defeats Go world champion Lee Sedol.

The duel man versus machine is over, and there is a clear winner: artificial intelligence. Lee Sedol did not expect the Google software to win - but he was proven wrong. The software's victory over the world's top-ranked Go player is a giant step in developing self-learning machines. The traditional Asian board game is even more complicated than chess and was previously considered a much more significant challenge for computer programs because there are significantly more potential moves. The AlphaGo program was trained using the Monte Carlo tree search algorithm, which finds previously-stored moves. All actions made in winning games were recorded and trained by both the computer and human players.

## The Drom Polytechnique team developed nanorobots in Montreal

The team developed these nanorobots as transporter robots that can deliver drugs and save surrounding organs and tissues. In one study, these nanorobots were used to provide an anti-cancer drug to oxygen-deprived cancer cells. These nanorobots were made using 100 million flagellating bacteria with a compass. Cancer drugs damage normal human cells, while the nanorobots minimized this drastic effect.

## The Microfluidic robot developed by Harvard University engineers

It was the first soft and autonomous microfluidic robot powered by a chemical reaction. It was made to serve small transparent impurities in the body. This robot did not require an electric circuit or batteries for charging.

# 2017

### BWIBots - The visionary robots

Researchers developed these visionary robots that leaned human performance. They worked with humans to learn how to cooperate on a specific task. BWI stands for Building-Wide Intelligence. This project's main goal was to design specific robots' attributes to train them to perform daily tasks in the home based on human interactions.

Commands are given using Natural Language Processing, and certain task windows were executed based on the training instructions

## Google Home Mini, a smart voice assistant for the home

Google Home Mini is a smaller yet advanced version of the Google Home speaker with a reasonable lower price, i.e. $49 versus $129. It is a voice-controlled speaker that can perform multiple tasks such as play music, control smart home gadgets, manage to-do lists, schedule calendars, play videos on Chromecast-enabled screens, add items to an online shopping cart, etc. Besides, you can now make calls and locate your phone if it has been misplaced somewhere in the house.

## Facebook's AI To Stop Suicide

Facebook's AI To Stop Suicide proactively plays at detecting suicidal status posts using AI, specifically Natural Language Processing (NLP), to scan and point out negative phrases of despair and hopelessness from users. This AI was presented with many negative and false positive phrases, and only negative emotional phrases were selected to train the software on real negative distress signals. When this proactive AI detects some suicidal intentions, it suddenly sends a message to the potential suicide's family and friends to cope with his situation.

# 2018

## The first AI robot CIMON is sent into space

The first AI robot, CIMON, is a head-sized AI-mediated robot developed by Airbus and IBM. It is the "Crew Interactive Mobile Companion." The fully voice-controlled robot, which includes camera and repair capabilities, was designed to reduce astronaut stress.

❀❀❀

## Lovot, the first emotional partner robot, developed by Groove X

With more than 50 sensors, LOVOT can sense your mood swings and act accordingly to change your mood from excited to agitated and peaceful. It has beautiful color-changing eyes and a warm body. It is more like a pet or a child controlled by a mobile app. You can buy this beautiful companion for only $3000.

## Facebook has started using computer vision AI to filter out explicit visual content

As the number of Facebook users grows, it becomes challenging to manually scan every post or shared file. Facebook has started using computer vision AI and image processing to check nudity and explicit graphics. Although there are many false positives, the application is evolving day by day until it becomes perfect.

❀❀❀

## Waymo One autonomous car launched by Waymo LLC

Waymo LLC is a self-driving car company under Alphabet LLC, a subsidiary of Google. In 2018, the Waymo One autonomous car was launched in the greater Pheonix, Arizona area. The core components of detection were sensors, lidars, 360-surveillance radars that can detect an object 300 meters away. Waymo engineers developed a virtual driving program called CarCraft to simulate driving behavior. By 2018, Waymo had driven 5 billion miles in the CarCraft world.

# 2019

### GPT-2 (with 1.5 billion parameters) is released.

Generative Pre-trained Transformer-2 (GPT-2) is a machine learning model for automatic text generation. Using NLP and Deep Learning can perform various text-related tasks such as question answering, summarization, and translation. It has 1.5 billion parameters (training set). It works amazingly well for short paragraphs but loses its meaning when generating longer sections. We have to give it a main statement; it can do the rest by itself.

### AI outperforms radiologists in diagnosing lung cancer

Researchers from GoogleAI and Langone Medical Center, Center for Biological Imaging, created a deep-learning algorithm that used past and currently computed tomography scans of lung cancer to predict lung cancer risk. In a comparative study, the AI outperformed six experienced radiologists in detecting potential lung cancer from scan reports. The AI model achieved 94% accuracy and a high reduction in scan reading time. The model successfully saw 6716 National Lung Cancer Screening Trial cases and 1139 validated cases, with the same accuracy (94%).

## Textron Systems launches Ripsaw M5 autonomous combat vehicle

The Ripsaw M5 Autonomous Battle Tank is fully automated, an electric battle tank that was unveiled at the Association of the U.S. Army expo in Washington, D.C. It is the most advanced intelligent combat vehicle with numerous programmable capabilities, including an adaptable turret, 260-degree surveillance and situational awareness system, and routine clearance options such as ground-penetrating radar, mine plow, IED knockdown roller, and mine-clearing line charge. It reaches a top speed of 65 MPH.

# 2020

## Microsoft introduces its Turing Natural Language Generation (T-NLG)

Turing Natural Language Generation (T-NLG) is a natural language generator with 17 billion parameters (it outperforms OpenAI's GPT-2). It can perform tasks such as free-form generation, question answering, sentence auto-completion, and paragraph summarization.

## Once-for-all model published by Han Cai and team

AI Edge devices produce a lot of carbon dioxide. One study found that training an off-the-shelf language processing system emits 1400 pounds of CO2. Training a fully processing AI from scratch can produce 78000 pounds of emissions. Han Cai and his team have developed an efficient algorithm for training networks once, namely the once-for-all model. In simpler terms, conventional AI systems train each data set according to a group of rules. Han Cai proposed to train an entire system once and then train the whole dataset without being trained from the beginning. This can save costs for the AI environment. The whole initiative is called "GreenAI," in which scientists are working to reduce the carbon footprint to run AI. The once-for-all model can reduce carbon emissions by 1300 times compared to traditional methods.

## OpenAI releases GPT-3 beta

Generative Pre-trained Transformer-3 (GPT-3) is a powerful AI model for natural language autoregression. It is considered the most amazing and feared AI model in NLP because of its ability to generate human-like text models. Some opponents believe that this model will contaminate text quality on the web, while proponents believe that machines will soon begin to speak. Given an initial set, this model completes upcoming phrases through Deep Learning from the web. Each training set can be called parameters, while the given model has 175 billion parameters. These parameters are optimized using neural networks. GPT-3 has proven that it is not only a language-generative model but can also generate HTML code, guitar nodes, and web pages.

## CurialAI, the first AI system to detect potential COVID-19 patients within an hour

Oxford University has developed an AI program, CurialAI, based on tests performed on hospital emergencies within an hour, such as blood tests and other vital signs. Core team members were Dr. Andrew Soltan of John Redcliffe Hospital, Professor David Clifton of the "AI for Health" Lab, and Professor David Eyre of the Oxford Big Data Institute. The AI training was launched in March 2020, and 115000 datasets have been fed into the program so far. Once trained, CurialAI distinguished between COVID and other respiratory patients within an hour (once clinical data was collected) with more than 90% accuracy.

## Waymo self-driving cars released to the public

It is the first autonomous car company to release driverless cars to the public. These Waymo Self-Driving Cars are available in the greater Phoenix, Arizona area with a full map. Users can download the app to their smartphone and hail the cab to their location. Previously, security guards accompanied the self-driving cars, but this is the first time a vehicle is driving without a human driver but as a passenger. Before the public launch, Waymo tested the self-driving car's capabilities with a simulation called CarCraft. Waymo drove 5 billion miles in a virtual world before hitting the road. Few accidents were reported during the driving tests, but most of them were errors by safety drivers or other cars. There was only one reported error where Waymo crashed into the side of a bus. Waymo's autonomous cars are ready for specific areas, but not the entire U.S.

## Google DeepMind's AlphaFold wins CASP Protein Folding Contest with the highest accuracy

Predicting protein structure is an essential part of drug design and understanding how life works. DeepMind's AlphaFold was initiated to understand protein structure best. In a CASP (Critical Assessment of Structure Prediction) competition, AlphaFold competed against 100 competitors and scored 87 points, while the second-best competitor scored 75 points. This was a remarkable achievement in computational biology. It will help develop new vaccines and drugs quickly and with the least side effects if the success continues.

## Soft robotic gripper similar to pole beans

At the University of Georgia, scientists have developed a small and sensitive soft robotic gripper that gently but securely holds smaller objects, even those as little as one millimeter in diameter. The gripper is only 3 inches long. This idea was adapted from pole beans that cling to a rope or other elongated structure. The process of making a soft robotic gripper required a single pneumatic controller to simplify its actions. The scientists also incorporated a fiber-optic sensor into the robot's flexible spine to sense the surface and writhe against the gripped object. This sensor also calculates the twin angle, the object's physical properties, and any external stimuli that may affect grasping.

# 2021

## Artificial Chemist 2.0

A group of researchers from North Carolina State University and the University at Buffalo has developed an intelligent robotic materials synthesizer to accelerate the design and fabrication of semiconductor nanomaterials for applications in next-generation photonic devices. This is the second generation of Artificial Chemist technology, i.e., a fluidic robo-chemist powered by an artificial intelligence (AI)-driven decision agent.

## Swinburne University of Technology Australia Researchers Introduced Neuromorphic Processor

Researchers from the Swinburne University of Technology in Australia and other continents have collaborated to unveil the world's fastest optical neuromorphic processor with a performance of 10 TeraOPs/s. This is the fastest processing speed ever achieved by a single processor. Other ultra processors, such as Google's TPUs, can perform 100 tera operations per second (TeraOPs/s), but thousands of parallel processors do this. Neuromorphic processors are modeled after the neural cortex of the human brain. The core structure of this processor consists of micro-combs (parallel array of high-quality infrared lasers). This allows AI scientists to train systems in neural networks, and even ultra-HD images can be processed with this new technology.

**Non-electronic robot born at the University of California.**

Soft robotics represents a new paradigm shift in robotics research. Unlike rigid robots, they offer flexibility and functionality in various environments. Most soft robots operate based on pneumatic circuits (compressed air and valves). However, the main problem is their brain circuitry, which is usually heavier and requires electricity. Michael T. Tolley and his team have developed a soft robot that uses pneumatic circuits consisting of tubes and soft valves. These circuits are embedded in the robot's body, making them lightweight and cheap. This robot can walk on command or move depending on the environment.

Currently, this robot is intended as a toy or to enter dungeons where other circuits do not work.

❦❦❦

**Nanotech scientists create the world's smallest origami nanorobot.**

The field of robotics continues to surprise us. Scientists at Cornell University have used a memory actuator to create a nanorobot that folds itself when powered by electricity. A shape memory alloy is used, meaning it bends when heat/current is applied and resumes its shape when the heat/voltage is removed. This concept has been used to make micron-sized origami birds that can fold, grasp objects under their folds, and move to a specific location. Programmable complementary metal oxide semi-conductor (CMOS) transistors were used to provide such a tiny robot with a brain. The team has already been nominated for the Guianese Book of World Records. But they are determined to achieve another milestone, a 60-micron nanorobot.

## Our adaptive immune system uses reinforcement learning against germs.

The adaptive immune system is our body's second line of defense. Soldiers are classified as either T cells or B cells. T cells are responsible for recognizing foreign pathogens and generating a response against them. So far, the biology of T-cells has been widely studied, but the recognition and training mechanisms have been unknown. This is where the role of artificial intelligence in healthcare came into play. The researchers used an artificial intelligence technique to find that T helper cells function like a hidden layer between input and output in neural networks. This approach is used in adaptive learning. In this scenario, pathogens/antigens are the input, and effector immune cells are the output. The team used simulation to understand the proposed mechanism of T cells. The results followed the experimental data on the sequence of T cell genes and proteins.

## Brain-computer interface records brain signals for handwriting.

Howard Hughes Medical Institute researchers have set up a brain-computer interface to record brain signals when a person thinks about writing a letter. This was a unique idea to record and replicate the expression of a paralyzed person who wants to write. First, the neural signal for each letter was recorded by giving instructions to the patient. After the patterns for all letters were recorded, the patient was asked to think of one letter. The signals recorded on the interface were found to be correct.

## MIT researchers have developed a self-sufficient microsystem.

This research is funded by the Army Research Laboratory of the U.S. Army Combat Capabilities Development Command. This project is a perfect example of using a living system to generate electricity. The system developed does not require a battery and can operate without human intervention. In addition, the same research team discovered that an air generator (or "air gene") based on protein nanowires could be used to generate electricity from the environment/humidity. These protein nanowires were extracted from Geobacter, capable of generating electricity from water vapor in the air. Air-Gen is connected to these nanowires to generate electricity. Interestingly, these nanowires can be used to make memristors, small brain-like devices for very low-power computation. Memristors are considered the children of neuromorphic processors.[4]

---

[4] The content of the achievements comes mostly from the website https://achievements.ai/

# What will be the next big achievement?

**We have only seen & experienced the tip of the iceberg regarding Artificial Intelligence.**

**An exciting but also challenging future with many unknown lies ahead.**

**Let's shape the future mindfully and sustainably for the good of humanity and nature.**

Thanks for reading

Murat

# APPENDIX: GLOSSARY

## Artificial intelligence

Artificial intelligence (AI) is intelligence exhibited by machines instead of the natural intelligence of humans and animals, which includes consciousness and emotionality. The distinction between the first and second categories is often made clear by the choice of an acronym. 'Strong' AI is usually referred to as AGI (Artificial General Intelligence), while attempts to emulate 'natural' intelligence are referred to as ABI (Artificial Biological Intelligence). Leading AI textbooks define the field as the study of "intelligent agents": any device that perceives its environment and performs actions that maximize its chance of successfully achieving its goals. Colloquially, the term "artificial intelligence" is often used to describe machines (or computers) that mimic "cognitive" functions that humans associate with the human mind, such as "learning" and "problem-solving."

# Artificial General Intelligence (Strong AI)

Artificial General Intelligence (AGI) is an intelligent agent's hypothetical ability to understand or learn any intellectual task that a human can. It is a primary goal of some artificial intelligence research and a common theme in science fiction and futurology. AGI may also be referred to as strong AI, full AI, or general intelligent action. Some academic sources reserve the term "strong AI" for computer programs that can experience sentience, self-awareness, and consciousness. It is speculated that today's AI is still decades away from AGI.

# Weak artificial intelligence (weak AI)

Weak artificial intelligence (weak AI) is an artificial intelligence that implements a limited part of the mind, or as narrow AI, is focused on a narrow task. In the words of John Searle, it would be "useful for testing hypotheses about the mind, but it would not really be mind." Contrast this with strong AI, which is defined as a machine capable of applying intelligence to any problem, rather than just a specific issue, which is sometimes considered a prerequisite for consciousness, sentience, and mind.

# The ethics of artificial intelligence

The ethics of artificial intelligence is the branch of technology ethics that deals specifically with artificially intelligent systems. It is sometimes divided into a concern with humans' moral behavior as they design, make, use, and treat artificially intelligent systems, and a problem with machines' behavior, machine ethics. It also includes the question of a possible singularity due to superintelligent AI.

# The European ethics guidelines for trustworthy AI[5]

On 8 April 2019, the High-Level Expert Group on AI presented Ethics Guidelines for Trustworthy Artificial Intelligence. This followed the publication of the guidelines' first draft in December 2018 on which more than 500 comments were received through an open consultation.

According to the Guidelines, trustworthy AI should be:

**(1) lawful - respecting all applicable laws and regulations**

---

[5] https://ec.europa.eu/digital-single-market/en/news/ethics-guidelines-trustworthy-ai

**(2) ethical - respecting ethical principles and values**

**(3) robust - both from a technical perspective while taking into account its social environment**

The Guidelines put forward a set of 7 key requirements that AI systems should meet in order to be deemed trustworthy. A specific assessment list aims to help verify the application of each of the key requirements:

**1. Human agency** and oversight: AI systems should empower human beings, allowing them to make informed decisions and fostering their fundamental rights. At the same time, proper oversight mechanisms need to be ensured, which can be achieved through human-in-the-loop, human-on-the-loop, and human-in-command approaches

**2. Technical Robustness and safety:** AI systems need to be resilient and secure. They need to be safe, ensuring a fall back plan in case something goes wrong, as well as being accurate, reliable and reproducible. That is the only way to ensure that also unintentional harm can be minimized and prevented.

**3. Privacy and data governance:** besides ensuring full respect for privacy and data protection, adequate data governance mechanisms must also be ensured, taking into account the quality and integrity of the data, and ensuring legitimized access to data.

**4. Transparency:** the data, system and AI business models should be transparent. Traceability mechanisms can help achieving this. Moreover, AI systems and their decisions should be explained in a manner adapted to the stakeholder concerned. Humans need to be aware that they are interacting with an AI system, and must be informed of the system's capabilities and limitations.

**5. Diversity, non-discrimination** and fairness: Unfair bias must be avoided, as it could could have multiple negative implications, from the marginalization of vulnerable groups, to the exacerbation of prejudice and discrimination. Fostering diversity, AI systems should be accessible to all, regardless of any disability, and involve relevant stakeholders throughout their entire life circle.

**6. Societal and environmental well-being:** AI systems should benefit all human beings, including future generations. It must hence be ensured that they are sustainable and environmentally friendly. Moreover, they should take into account the environment, including other living beings, and their social and societal impact should be carefully considered.

**7. Accountability:** Mechanisms should be put in place to ensure responsibility and accountability for AI systems and their outcomes. Auditability, which enables the assessment of algorithms, data and design processes plays a key role therein, especially in critical applications. Moreover, adequate an accessible redress should be ensured.

# Algorithmic bias

Algorithmic bias describes systematic and repeatable errors in a computer system that lead to unfair results, such as favoring one arbitrary group of users over others. Discrimination can occur due to many factors, including but not limited to the algorithm's design or the unintended or unanticipated use or decisions regarding how data is coded, collected, selected, or used to train the algorithm. Algorithmic bias occurs across platforms, including but not limited to search engine results and social media platforms, and can have effects ranging from unintentional privacy violations to reinforcing social biases related to race, gender, sexuality, and ethnicity. The study of algorithmic bias focuses primarily on algorithms that reflect "systematic and unfair" discrimination. This bias has only recently been addressed in legal frameworks such as the 2018 European Union General Data Protection Regulation. More comprehensive regulation is needed as new technologies become more advanced and opaquer.

# Machine Learning

Machine learning (ML) is the study of computer algorithms that improve automatically through experience. It is considered a part of artificial intelligence. Machine learning algorithms build a model based on sample data, called "training data," to make predictions or decisions without being explicitly programmed to do so. Machine learning algorithms are used in various applications, such as email filtering and computer vision, where it is difficult or infeasible to develop traditional algorithms to perform the required tasks.

# Deep Learning

Deep learning is a class of machine learning algorithms that uses multiple layers to progressively extract higher-level features from raw input. In image processing, for example, lower layers can detect edges, while higher layers identify concepts relevant to a human, such as digits, letters, or faces.

# Supervised learning

Supervised learning is the machine learning task of learning a function that maps an input to an output, based on exemplar input-output pairs. It infers a process from labeled training data consisting of a set of training examples. In supervised learning, each sample is a pair consisting of an input object (usually a vector) and the desired output value (also called a supervisory signal). A supervised learning algorithm analyzes the training data and produces a derived function that can be used to map new examples. An optimal scenario allows the algorithm to correctly determine the class labels for unseen instances. This requires that the learning algorithm generalizes from training data to unseen situations in a "reasonable" way.

This statistical quality of an algorithm is measured by the so-called generalization error.

# Unsupervised learning

Unsupervised learning is a type of algorithm that learns patterns from unlabeled data. The hope is that imitation will force the machine to build a compact internal representation of its world. Unlike supervised learning (SL), where data is tagged by a human, e.g., as "car" or "fish," etc., UL exhibits self-organization, capturing patterns as neural preselections or probability densities. The other stages in the supervision spectrum are reinforcement learning. The machine receives only a numerical performance score for guidance and semi-supervised learning. A smaller portion of the data is tagged. Two widely used methods in UL are neural networks and probabilistic methods.

# Semi-supervised learning

Semi-supervised learning is a machine learning approach in which a small amount of tagged data is combined with a large amount of unlabeled data during training. Semi-supervised learning lay between unsupervised learning (without labeled training data) and supervised learning (with labeled training data only). It is a particular case of weak supervision.

# Reinforcement learning

Reinforcement learning is an area of machine learning that deals with how intelligent agents should perform actions in an environment to maximize the notion of cumulative reward. Reinforcement learning is one of the three fundamental paradigms of machine learning, supervised learning and unsupervised learning.

# Superintelligence

A superintelligence is a hypothetical agent that possesses intelligence far exceeding that of the brightest and most gifted human minds. "Superintelligence" can also refer to a property of problem-solving systems (e.g., superintelligent language translators or technical assistants), whether or not these high-level intellectual competencies are embodied in agents operating in the world. A superintelligence may or may not arise from an intelligence explosion and be associated with a technological singularity.

# Technological Singularity

The technological Singularity - or merely the Singularity - is a theoretical point when technological growth becomes uncontrollable and irreversible, leading to unpredictable changes in human civilization. According to the most popular version of the singularity hypothesis, called the intelligence explosion, an upgradable intelligent agent will eventually enter a "run-through reaction" of self-improvement cycles. Each new and more intelligent generation at an increasing rate will emerge, resulting in an intelligence "explosion." A powerful superintelligence emerges, far surpassing all human intelligence in quality.

# The Philosophy of Artificial Intelligence

Artificial intelligence is a branch of the philosophy of technology that deals with artificial intelligence and its implications for knowledge and understanding of intelligence, ethics, consciousness, epistemology, and free will. Besides, engineering is concerned with creating artificial animals or artificial humans, so the discipline is of considerable interest to philosophers. These factors contributed to the emergence of the philosophy of artificial intelligence. Some scholars argue that the rejection of philosophy by the AI community is detrimental.

The philosophy of artificial intelligence attempts to answer questions such as the following:

• Can a machine act intelligently?

• Can it solve any problem that a human would solve by thinking?

• Are human intelligence and machine intelligence the same thing?

• Is the human brain practically a computer?

• Can a machine have a mind, mental states, and consciousness in the same sense as humans?

• Can it sense how things are?

Questions like these reflect the divergent interests of AI researchers, cognitive scientists, and philosophers, respectively. The scientific answers to these questions depend on how "intelligence" and "consciousness" are defined and on exactly which "machines" are under discussion.

# AI Control Problem

In artificial intelligence (AI) and philosophy, the AI control problem is how to build a superintelligent agent that helps its creators and avoids accidentally building a superintelligence that harms its creators. Its investigation is motivated by the notion that humanity must solve the control problem before any superintelligence is created. A poorly designed superintelligence could rationally decide to control its environment and refuse to allow its creators to change it after launch. Also, some scientists argue that solutions to the control problem, among other advances in AI safety technology, could find application in existing non-superintelligent AI.

Critical approaches to the control problem include alignment, which aims to align AI target systems with human values, and capability control, aiming to reduce an AI system's ability to harm humans or gain power. Capability control proposals are generally not reliable or sufficient to solve the control problem but rather as a potentially valuable complement to alignment efforts.

# The Turing Test

The Turing Test, originally called the Imitation Game by Alan Turing in 1950, is a test of a machine's ability to exhibit intelligent behavior equivalent to or indistinguishable from a human. Turing proposed that a human rater evaluate natural language conversations between humans and a machine designed to produce human-like responses. The rater would be aware that one of the two interlocutors is a machine, and all participants would be separate from each other. The conversation would be limited to a text-only channel such as a computer keyboard and screen so that the score would not depend on the machine's ability to render words as speech. If the tester cannot reliably distinguish the device from a human, the test is considered passed. The test results do not depend on the machine's ability to give correct answers to questions but only how closely its solutions resemble those of a human.